The Story of the Christian Church

HENRY IV WHO STOOD BAREFOOTED THREE DAYS IN THE SNOW AT
CANOSSA AWAITING ADMITTANCE TO POPE GREGORY VII.   (See page 111.)

The Story of the Christian Church

Jesse Lyman Hurlbut, D. D.

Author of

HURLBUT'S STORY OF THE BIBLE

New and Revised Edition

ZONDERVAN PUBLISHING HOUSE
GRAND RAPIDS, MICHIGAN

PREFACE

Never in all of recorded history has there been a greater need for religion than at the present time. Enlightened by knowledge gained through science— benefited by the strides in technocracy, modern man stands bewildered that good will on earth has never been further from accomplishment. Yet the reason is a simple one—and obvious. There is no real enlightenment, no lasting benefits, unless achievement springs from a soil in which the seed of the spirit is also planted. Spiritual values have been torn up and cast about as if they were weeds preventing the growth of progress. The result is chaos. Men are beginning to again turn to religion where truths have stood the test of time.

In a volume of only a few hundred pages, the Story of the Christian Church can be told only by the most careful selectivity. The controversies over abstruse doctrines which swept successively over the Church and rent it asunder mostly seem to our time of little worth. In this handbook the spirit of the Church, the stream of its tendency, the causes leading to historic events and the events flowing from them have been made the center of interest.

Two different constituencies have been kept steadily in view during the preparation of this volume, and the effort has been made to adapt it to the desires of both elements. As a textbook for students, either as individuals or in classes, or for communicants desiring knowledge of the Church's history, it has been carefully outlined; the divisions and subdivisions have been stated in detail before the account of each general period; and to each period is given a carefully selected list of books serviceable to either teachers or pupils who may desire a larger knowledge of the subject. At the end of the book may be found a blackboard outline and review questions covering each chapter.

But, besides students, there are readers to be provided for. The outlines and references have been arranged upon the margin, and do not appear in the text. It has been sought to give in the book a smooth narrative, unbroken by topic-heads, so that it may be read continuously as an interesting story. The outline can be found by the reader who desires to follow it, but it is not thrust upon him. The aim has been to supply a book accurate in all its statements, calling attention to great events and great leaders, and at the same time in a style that may be interesting and attractive.

TABLE OF CONTENTS.

OUTLINE OF CHAPTERS I, II, III, IV, V.

I. THE APOSTOLIC CHURCH.
From the Ascension of Christ, 30 A. D.,
To the Death of St. John, 100 A. D.

II. THE PERSECUTED CHURCH.
From the Death of St. John, 100 A. D.,
To the Edict of Constantine, 313 A. D.

III. THE IMPERIAL CHURCH.
From the Edict of Constantine, 313 A. D.,
To the Fall of Rome, 476 A. D.

IV. THE MEDIEVAL CHURCH.
From the Fall of Rome, 476 A. D.,
To the Fall of Constantinople, 1453 A. D.

V. THE REFORMED CHURCH.
From the Fall of Constantinople, 1453 A. D.,
To the End of the Thirty Years' War, 1648 A. D.

VI. THE MODERN CHURCH.
From the End of the Thirty Years' War, 1648 A. D.,
To the Twentieth Century, 1901 A. D.

FIRST GENERAL PERIOD. THE APOSTOLIC CHURCH.

From the Ascension of Christ, 30 A. D.,
To the Death of St. John, 100 A. D.

I. THE PENTECOSTAL CHURCH (CHAPTER II)

From the Ascension of Christ, 30 A. D.,
To the Preaching of Stephen, 35 A. D.

1. Definition of the Church.
2. Its Beginning. The Day of Pentecost, 30 A. D.
3. Its Endowment. The Holy Spirit.
    (1) Illuminating.
    (2) Empowering.
    (3) Abiding.
4. Its Locality. The City of Jerusalem.
5. Its Membership.
    (1) Hebrews.
    (2) Grecian Jews or Hellenists.
    (3) Proselytes.

6. Its Leaders: St. Peter, St. John.
7. Its Government, by the Twelve Apostles.
8. Its Doctrines.
    (1) The Messiahship of Jesus.
    (2) The Resurrection of Jesus.
    (3) The Return of Jesus.
9. Its Gospel Testimony.
10. Its Miracles.
11. Its Spirit of Brotherhood. "Community of Property." (?)
    (1) Voluntary.
    (2) Small Community.
    (3) Selected People.
    (4) Expecting Christ's Return.
    (5) A Financial Failure.
    (6) Developing Moral Evils.
12. The One Defect of the Pentecostal Church—Its Lack of Missionary Zeal.

II. THE EXPANDING CHURCH, 35-50 A. D. (CHAPTER III).

From the Preaching of Stephen, 35 A. D.,

To the Council at Jerusalem, 50 A. D.

1. Stephen's Preaching.
2. Saul's Persecution.
3. Philip in Samaria.
4. Peter at Joppa and Cæsarea.
5. Saul's Conversion.
6. The Church at Antioch.
7. The First Missionary Journey.
    (1) Two Workers in Unison.
    (2) A Younger Man as Helper.
    (3) Large Cities as Fields of Labor.
    (4) Beginning in the Synagogue.
    (5) Revisiting the Churches Founded.
8. The Council at Jerusalem, 50 A. D.

III. THE CHURCH AMONG THE GENTILES, A. D. 50-68 (CHAPTER IV).

From the Council at Jerusalem, 50 A. D.,

To the Martyrdom of St. Paul, 68 A. D.

1. Authorities.
2. Field.
3. Members.
4. Leaders: St. Paul, St. Peter, St. James.
5. Missionary Journeys of St. Paul.
    (1) The Second Journey. Europe Visited.
    (2) The Third Journey. The Church at Ephesus.
    (3) The Fourth Journey. Paul a Prisoner.
6. The First Imperial Persecution. (Nero.)
7. Literature of the Period.

IV. THE AGE OF SHADOWS, 68-100 A. D. (CHAPTER V).

From the Martyrdom of St. Paul, 68 A. D.,
To the Death of St. John, 100 A. D.

1. The Fall of Jerusalem, 70 A. D.
2. The Second Imperial Persecution (Domitian), 90 A. D.
3. The Completion of the New Testament.
4. The Condition of the Church.
   (1) Extent and Numbers.
   (2) Doctrinal System.
   (3) Institutions: (a) Baptism.   (b) The Lord's Day.   (c) The Lord's Supper.   (d) Easter Sunday.
   (4) Its Officers: (a) Apostles.   (b) Elders or Bishops.   (c) Deacons.
   (5) Its Worship.
   (6) Its Spiritual State.

WORKS FOR FURTHER STUDY.

Read the Book of Acts.
Landmarks of Church History. Henry Cowan.   Chaps. I, II.
The Story of the Christian Centuries. E. G. Selden.   Chap. I.
History and Literature of the Early Church. James Orr. Chaps. I-IV.
The Life and Work of St. Paul.   F. W. Farrar.
Compendium of Church History. A. C. Zenos.   Chaps. I, II.
Epochs of Church History—The Apostolic Age.   J. V. Bartlett.
The Apostolic Age. O. J. Thatcher.
A Short History of the Christian Church. J. W. Moncrief. Chap. I.
The Early Days of Christianity. F. W. Farrar.
History of the Christian Church. G. P. Fisher. Pp. 1-44.
History of the Christian Church. J. F. Hurst. Vol I, pp. 61-148.
History of the Christian Church. Philip Schaff. Vol. I.
Darkness and Dawn. F. W. Farrar. (Fiction.)
Quo Vadis. H. Sienkiewicz. (Fiction.)

The Story of the Christian Church

CHAPTER I.

THE SIX GENERAL PERIODS OF CHURCH HISTORY.

Before we enter upon a detailed study of the nineteen centuries through which the Church of Christ has been at work, let us take our stand upon a mountain-top of vision, and view, as in a landscape, the entire field which, step by step, we are to traverse. From the view-point of today, in this amazing twentieth century, we look back and see rising, here and there above the plains of time, like successive peaks, the great events of Christian history, which serve as points of division, each marking the end of one epoch and the beginning of another. We count these turning-points, and find them six in number, indicating the Six Great Periods in the history of the church. Let us in this opening chapter take a general view of these periods.

The height which marks the starting-point of the Church of Christ is the Mount of Olives, just outside the eastern wall of Jerusalem. Here, about the year 30 A. D., Jesus Christ, newly risen from his tomb in the garden, gave his last commands, and then ascended to his heavenly throne. We see a little company of Jewish believers in their departed Lord as the Messiah-King of Israel, tarrying for a

Period I. The Apostolic Church. From the Ascension of Christ, 30 A. D.,

time in Jerusalem, at first with no thought of a church outside the bounds of Judaism; gradually widening their views and their ministry until their vision embraced the winning of the world to Christ. Under the leadership of St. Peter, St. Paul and their immediate successors the church was established within two generations in nearly every land from the Euphrates to the Tiber, and from the Black Sea to the River Nile. The first period ends with the death of St. John, the last of the twelve apostles upon earth, which is said to have taken place about 100 A. D. This epoch we call "The Period of the Apostolic Church."

To the Death of St. John, 100 A. D.

For more than two hundred years succeeding the Apostolic Age we look upon the church under the sword of persecution. During all the second century, all the third century, and in the early years of the fourth century, the mightiest empire upon earth invoked all its power to destroy what was called "the Christian superstition." For seven generations a noble army of martyrs, by the hundred thousand, won their crowns through the axe, the wild beasts in the arena, and the fiery stake. Yet, in the face of the most relentless persecution, the followers of Christ increased in number, until they counted, in public or in secret, nearly if not quite half the population of the Roman Empire. At last a Christian emperor sat upon the throne and by his edict stayed the tide of slaughter.

Period II.

The Persecuted Church.

From the Death of St. John, 100 A. D.,

To the Edict of Constantine, 313 A. D.

Apparently the Christians, so long oppressed, at one step passed from the prison to the throne; for the Persecuted Church became the Imperial Church.

Period III.

The Imperial Church.

The cross took the place of the eagle as the standard of the nation, and Christianity was made the religion of the Roman empire. A Christian capital, Constantinople, arose and displaced old Rome; but Rome as it ceased to be heathen began to arise as the capital of the church. The western Roman Empire was overwhelmed by barbarian hordes, but these conquerors were conquered by the church, and founded not heathen but Christian nations in Europe. *From the Edict of Constantine, 313 A. D., To the Fall of Rome, 476 A. D.*

With the fall of the western Roman Empire begins the period of a thousand years, known as the Middle Ages. At its opening we see Europe in chaos, a continent of tribes uncontrolled by any central power, but gradually shaping themselves into kingdoms; we see the Roman bishop, as pope, endeavoring to dominate not only the church but the world; we see the religion and empire of Mohammed conquering all the lands of early Christianity; we see the Holy Roman Empire established, and its emperors warring with the popes; we watch the romantic movement of the Crusades, in the vain endeavor to wrest the Holy Land from its Moslem masters; we see the awakening of Europe with the promise of a coming reformation in the new age. As ancient history ends with the fall of Rome, so medieval history ends with the fall of Constantinople. *Period IV. The Medieval Church. From the Fall of Rome, 476 A. D., To the Fall of Constantinople, 1453 A. D.*

After the fifteenth century with the awakening of Europe, came the sixteenth century with the reformation of the church. We behold Martin Luther nailing his declaration upon the cathedral *Period V. The Reformed Church.*

door; making his defense before the emperor and
the nobles of Germany; and rending shackles from
the consciences of men. We see the Church of Rome
shorn in twain by the peoples of northern Europe
breaking away and establishing their own national
churches of a purer type. But we see also a counter-
reformation begun in the Catholic lands, staying
the progress of reform; until at last after the ter-
rors of a thirty years' civil war in Germany, by the
Peace of Westphalia, in 1648, the lines are perma-
nently drawn between the Roman Catholic and the
Protestant nations.

Period VI.
The
Modern
Church.
From the
End of the
Thirty Years'
War, 1648,
We shall pass in rapid review the great movements that have stirred the churches and the people
in the last three centuries, in England, on the continent of Europe, and in America: the Puritan, the
Wesleyan, the Rationalistic, the Anglo-Catholic,
and the modern missionary movements, which have
contributed to the building up of the church of our
own time, and have made it, notwithstanding its
myriad forms and names, one church throughout
the world. We shall notice also the great change
which has gradually transformed the Christianity
in the nineteenth and twentieth centuries, into a
mighty organization, not only for the glory of God
but for the service of men, in reforms, in social
uplifting, in active efforts for the betterment of
mankind.

CHAPTER II.

THE PENTECOSTAL CHURCH.

FROM THE ASCENSION OF CHRIST, 30 A. D., TO THE
PREACHING OF STEPHEN, 35 A. D.

The Christian Church in every age, past, present, and to come, consists of all who believe in Jesus of Nazareth as the Son of God, who accept him as their personal Saviour from sin, and who obey him as the Christ, the Prince of the Kingdom of God on earth. *1. Definition of the Church.*

The Church of Christ began its history as a world movement on the Day of Pentecost, in the late spring of the year 30 A. D., fifty days after the Resurrection of our Lord, and ten days after his Ascension. During the ministry of Jesus, his disciples believed that he was the long-looked-for Messiah of Israel, the Christ. These two words are the same, "Messiah" being Hebrew, and "Christ" being Greek: and both meaning, "The Anointed One," the Prince of the Heavenly Kingdom. But although Jesus accepted this title from his immediate followers, he forbade them to proclaim this truth to the people in general until after he should rise from the dead; and during the forty days following his resurrection he commanded them, before beginning to preach his gospel to wait for the *2. Its Beginning.* *Matt. 16:20.*

baptism of the Holy Spirit; after which experience they were to be his witnesses throughout the world.

Acts 1:6-8.

3. Its Endowment. Acts 1:15. Acts 2:1-4.

On the morning of the Day of Pentecost, while all the followers of Jesus, in number one hundred and twenty, were assembled in their place of meeting, and praying, the Holy Spirit came upon them in a marvelous manner.   So vivid was the manifestation that tongues of flame were seen to fall from above and to rest upon the heads of all present. The effect of this experience was three-fold; it illuminated their minds, giving them a new view of the Kingdom of God, that it was not a political empire, but a spiritual realm, with their ascended Lord as its invisible yet active ruler over the hearts of those who accepted him by faith; it empowered them, bestowing upon every member a fervor of spirit and a power of utterance which made their testimony convincing to those who heard it; and this divine spirit has dwelt in the church from that day as an abiding presence; not in its organization or machinery, but as the personal, individual possession of every true believer according to the proportion of each member's faith and consecration. From the outpouring of the spirit on that day, the birthday of the Christian Church, the fellowship of those earliest years has been rightly named The Pentecostal Church.

Effects. (1) Illuminating.

(2) Empowering.

(3) Abiding.

I Cor. 3:16. Eph. 2:21, 22.

4. Its Locality.

The church began in the city of Jerusalem, and apparently was limited to that city and its immediate surroundings during the earliest years of its history.   Throughout the land, and especially in the northern province of Galilee, were groups of people who believed in Jesus as the Messiah-King, but no record has reached us of their organization and recognition as branches of the church. The upper room on Mount Zion, and Solomon's porch in the Temple were the headquarters of the church throughout its earliest epoch.

All the members of the Pentecostal Church were Jews; and, so far as we can perceive, none of the members, or even of the apostolic company, at first dreamed that Gentiles would ever be admitted to membership. They may have supposed that the heathen world would at some time first become Jewish, and then accept Jesus as the Christ. The Jews of that age were of three classes, and all were represented in the Jerusalem Church. The Hebrews were those whose ancestors for generations had dwelt in Palestine, and were of pure Israelite race. Their language was called "the Hebrew tongue," which in the process of the centuries had been changed from the classic Hebrew of the Old Testament into what has been named an Aramaic or Syro-Chaldaic dialect. The Scriptures were read in the synagogues in the ancient Hebrew, but were translated by an interpreter, sentence by sentence, into the popular speech. The Grecian Jews or Hellenists were Jews descended from "the diaspora or dispersion;" that is Jews, whose home or whose ancestry was in foreign lands. Many of these had settled in Jerusalem and Judea, and synagogues had been established for their varied nationalities. After the conquest of the East by Alexander the Great, the Greek language became the prevailing tongue among

5. Its Membership.

(1) Hebrews
Acts 6:1.

Acts 21:40.

(2) Hellenists.

Acts 2:9-11

Acts 6:9.

330 B. C.

all the lands east of the Adriatic Sea, and to a
large degree even in Rome and throughout Italy,
and on this account the Jews of foreign ancestry
were called "Grecians" or "Hellenists," the word
"Hellen" meaning "a Greek." The Hellenists as
a people, especially outside of Palestine, were by
far the more numerous, the more wealthy, the more
intelligent, and the more liberal branch of the
Jewish race.   Proselytes were people of foreign
blood who had renounced heathenism, embraced the
Jewish law, and entered the Jewish Church by
receiving the rite of circumcision.   Although a
minority among the Jewish people, they were to be
found in many synagogues throughout the cities of
the Roman empire, and enjoyed all the privileges of
Jews.   The proselytes are to be distinguished from
"the devout" or "God-fearers," who were Gentiles
that had ceased to worship idols, and attended the
synagogue, but had not undergone circumcision,
did not undertake to observe the minute requirements of Jewish rules, and were not counted among
Jews, though friendly to them.

A reading of the first six chapters in the Book of
Acts will show that during this early period the
apostle Simon Peter was the leader of the church.
On every occasion Peter comes to the front as the
planner, the preacher, the wonder-worker, and the
defender of the infant church.   This was not because
Peter was the divinely-appointed pope or ruler;
but as the result of his promptness in decision, his
readiness of speech and his spirit of leadership.
By the side of Peter the practical we see John the

(3) Prose-
lytes.
Acts 6:5.

6. Its
Leaders.

contemplative and the spiritual, rarely speaking yet
ever held in high honor by the believers.

In a church of comparatively small numbers, 7. Its Gov-
all in one city, all of one race, all absolutely obedi- ernment.
ent to the will of their ascended Lord, and all in
fellowship with the Spirit of God, little government
was needed; but that little was given by the twelve
apostles as a body, Peter being their spokesman.
A sentence in Acts 5:13, intimates the reverence in
which the apostles were held, both by the believers
and the people.

At first, the church had a simple theology or 8. Its Doc-
body of belief. Systematic doctrine was developed trines.
later in the mind of St. Paul. But we can see in the
discourses of Peter three doctrines standing out
prominently, and held as essential. First and (1) Jesus the
greatest was the Messiahship of Jesus; that Jesus Messiah.
of Nazareth was the Messiah, the Christ, long
expected by Israel, and now reigning over his kingdom though invisible in the heavens; to whom each
member of the church was expected to give personal
loyalty, reverence, and obedience. Another essential doctrine was the Resurrection of Jesus; that (2) The
he had been crucified, had risen from the dead, Resurrection
and was now living, the head of his church, to of Jesus.
die no more. The third of these cardinal doctrines
was that of the Return of Jesus; that he who had (3) The
ascended to heaven was in due time to come back Return
to earth and reign over his church. Although of Jesus.
Jesus had told his disciples that of the time of his Matt. 24:36.
return to earth no man, nor angel, not even the Son
himself, but only the Father knew; yet the expecta-

I Thess. 4:15-17.

tion was general that his coming would be soon, even to that generation.

9. Its Gospel Testimony.

The weapon of the church through which the world was to be won, was the testimony of its members. As we have on record reports of several discourses by Peter, and none during this period by other disciples, we might suppose that Peter was the only preacher. But a close reading of the history shows that all the apostles, and all the church gave their testimony to the gospel. When the church had one hundred and twenty members, and the spirit descended upon them, all became preach-Acts 2:4, 11, 17, 18.ers of the word. As the numbers were multiplied, the witnesses multipled, for every member spoke as a messenger of Christ, there being no distinction between clergy and laity. Toward the close of this period, we find Stephen rising to such eminence as a preacher, that even the apostles are less prominent. This universal testimony was a potent influence in the rapid increase of the church.

10. Its Miracles.

In the beginning of this mighty effort, a handful of plain people, without arms or social prestige, and with all the powers of the national church and state arrayed against them, undertaking to transform a nation,—some supernatural help was needed; and it came in the form of "mighty works." The apostolic miracles have been named "bells to call Acts 3:1-8.the people to worship." We read of a work of healing wrought at the Beautiful Gate of the Temple, immediately followed by a multitude of people listening to Peter and submitting to Christ. There is the record of a miracle of judgment, the sudden deaths of Ananias and Sapphira at Peter's rebuke, Acts 5·1-12. as a warning against selfishness and falsehood. We read again of an efflorescence of divine power, in the cure of many diseased people. Nor was this Acts 5:12-26 power limited to Peter or the apostles; there is mention of "wonders and signs" wrought by Acts 6:8. Stephen. These mighty works attracted attention, awakened enquiry, and opened the hearts of multitudes to faith in Christ.

The love of Christ glowing in the hearts of these 11. Its Spirit of Brotherhood. people called forth also a love for their fellow-disciples, an unity of spirit, a joy in fellowship, and especially a self-denying interest in the needy members of the church. We read of a surrender of Acts 2:44, 45; 4:32-37. property on the part of the richer disciples so general as to suggest the extreme of socialism in a community of goods.* But concerning this aspect of "Community of Property."(?) the Pentecostal Church it should be noted that it (1) Voluntary. was entirely voluntary, not under the compulsion of law, not the poor demanding the property of the rich, but the rich of their own accord giving to the poor; that it was tested in a small community, all (2) Small Community. dwelling within one city; and in a highly-selected people, all filled with the Holy Spirit, in character (3) Select People. aiming to reproduce the principles of the Sermon on the Mount; that it arose in the expectation of a speedy return of Christ, at whose coming earthly (4) Expecting Christ's Return. possessions might be no longer needed; that as a financial experiment it was a failure, soon abandoned, (5) Financial Failure. and leaving the church in Jerusalem so poor that for

---

* These suggestions are condensed from a discourse of Dean Charles R. Brown, of the Yale Divinity School.

Acts 11:29.
Rom. 15:25,
26.
(6) Moral
Evils.

a generation collections were taken abroad for its relief; also, that the system developed its own moral evils, as the selfishness of Ananias and Sapphira. We are still on the earth, and need the spur of self-interest and of necessity. The spirit of this liberal giving is to be commended, but its plan may have been unwise.

12. Its One
Defect.

In almost every aspect the church of the first days was faultless. It was strong in faith and testimony, pure in character, and abundant in love. But its one defect was its lack of missionary zeal. It stayed at home, when it should have gone abroad with the gospel to other lands and other peoples. It needed the stimulus of sharp persecution to send it forth on its world-wide mission; and that stimulus it soon received.

CHAPTER III.

THE EXPANDING CHURCH.

FROM THE PREACHING OF STEPHEN, 35 A. D., TO
THE COUNCIL AT JERUSALEM, 50 A. D.

We now enter upon an epoch in the history of the Christian Church, which, although brief—only fifteen years, from about 35 to 50 A. D.—is of paramount importance. At that time was settled the great question, whether Christianity should remain an obscure Jewish sect, or should become a church wide open to all the world. When this brief period began the gospel was limited to the city of Jerusalem and the villages around it, and every member was an Israelite either by birth or adoption. When it ended, the church was deeply planted in Syria and Asia Minor, and was reaching out toward Europe. Also, its membership was no longer exclusively Jewish, but was predominantly Gentile. The language spoken in its assemblies in Palestine was Hebrew or Aramaic, but in a far wider area Greek was the tongue of its people. Let us notice the successive stages in this expanding movement.

Importance of the Epoch.

Stages of Expansion.

A complaint was heard in the church at Jerusalem, that in the distribution of the funds for the poor, the families of the Grecian Jews or Hellenists were

1. Stephen's Preaching.

Acts 6:1-4.

(27)

neglected.   The apostles called the church together, and proposed that a board of seven men be chosen for this service.   This plan was adopted, and of the seven men appointed, the first named was Stephen, "a man full of faith and of the Holy Spirit." Although chosen for a secular work, Stephen soon attracted notice as a preacher.   From the accusation against him when he was arrested by the Jewish rulers, and from the tenor of his address at his trial, it is evident that Stephen proclaimed Jesus as a Saviour not only for Jews, but also for Gentiles of every nation.   Stephen was the first in the church to have the vision of a world-wide gospel; and it was that which caused him to be the first Christian martyr.

Among those who heard Stephen, and were aroused to anger by his utterances, thoroughly repugnant to the Jewish mind, was a young man from Tarsus, on the coast of Asia Minor, named Saul.   He had been educated in Jerusalem under the great Gamaliel and was an accredited rabbi or teacher of the Jewish law.   Saul took part in the slaying of Stephen and, immediately after his death,' became the leader in a persecution of the disciples of Christ, seizing, binding, and scourging both men and women.   The Jerusalem Church was broken up for the time, and its members scattered abroad. But wherever they went, to Samaria, to Damascus, or even as far as Antioch in Syria, they became preachers of the gospel, and established churches. Thus did the fiery hate of Saul prove an aid to the expansion of the church.

Acts 6:5

Acts 6:11-14.

Acts 7:1-53.

Acts 7:57-60.

2. Saul's Persecution. Acts 7:58.

Acts 22:3.

Acts 8:3. Acts 26:9-11.

Acts 11:19, 20.

Acts 8:4.

In the list of the seven men associated with Stephen in the stewardship of the gifts for the poor, we find the name of Philip, who is to be distinguished from another Philip, one of the apostles. After the death of Stephen, Philip found refuge among the Samaritans, a mixed people, who were neither Jews nor Gentiles but held in contempt by the Jews. That Philip should begin preaching to Samaritans showed his freedom from the narrow Jewish spirit. In Samaria Philip established a church, which was duly recognized by the apostles Peter and John; the first church outside the pale of Judaism, yet not quite a church of Gentile members. Philip after this preached and founded churches in the coast cities of Gaza, Joppa, and Cæsarea. These were Gentile cities, but all having a large Jewish population. Here the gospel would of necessity come into contact with the heathen world.

In his journeys for the supervision of the church, Peter came to Joppa, on the seacoast. Here he raised to life Tabitha or Dorcas, and stayed for a time with another Simon, who was a tanner. His abiding with a tanner would show that Peter was already emancipated from the strict rules of Jewish custom; for men of that trade were ceremonially "unclean." Here a vision came to the apostle, of a great sheet let down from above, containing all kinds of animals; and a voice spoke to Peter, "What God hath cleaned, that call not thou common." Immediately afterward messengers arrived from Cæsarea, thirty miles to the north, asking

3. Philip in Samaria.
Acts 6:5.

Acts 8:5-13.

Acts 8:14-17.

Acts 8:40.

4. Peter at Joppa and Cæsarea.
Acts 9:32-43.

Acts 10:9-16.

Acts 10:17-48.

for Peter to come and instruct Cornelius, a devout Roman officer. Under direction of the Spirit Peter went to Cæsarea, preached the gospel to Cornelius and his friends, and received them into the church by baptism: the Spirit of God testifying divine approval by an outpouring, similar to that on the Day of Pentecost. Thus a divine sanction was given to preaching the gospel to Gentiles and their acceptance in the church.

5. Saul's Conversion. Acts 9:1-22. About this time, possibly just before Peter's visit to Cæsarea, Saul, the persecutor, was arrested on his way to Damascus by a vision of the ascended Jesus, and he who had been the most dreaded antagonist of the gospel now became its most powerful advocate. His opposition had been especially bitter against a doctrine which leveled the barriers between Jews and Gentiles, but, when converted, Saul at once adopted Stephen's views, and was a greater than Stephen in carrying onward the movement for a church open to all men, whether Jews or Gentiles. In all the history of Christianity no single conversion to Christ carried with it such momentous results to the whole world, as that of Saul the persecutor, afterward Paul the Apostle.

6. The Church at Antioch. Acts 11:19-29. In the persecution which began with the slaying of Stephen, the church at Jerusalem was scattered widely. Some of its members escaped to Damascus, others fled three hundred miles to Antioch, the capital of Syria, of which great province Palestine was a part. At Antioch these fugitives went into the Jewish synagogue, and there gave their testimony for Jesus as the Messiah. In every synagogue a place was set apart for Gentile worshipers; many of these heard the gospel at Antioch and embraced the faith of Christ; so that in that city a church grew up wherein Jews and Gentiles worshiped together as equals in privilege.   When news of this condition reached Jerusalem, the mother church was alarmed and sent a representative to examine this relation with the Gentiles. Fortunately, the choice of a delegate fell upon Barnabas, the broad-minded, open-hearted, and generous. He went to Antioch, and instead of condemning the church for its liberality rejoiced in it, endorsed the movement, and stayed at Antioch to participate in it. Barnabas had shown his confidence in Saul before; now he went to Saul's home in Tarsus, about a hundred miles from Antioch, mostly by water, brought Saul with him to Antioch, and made him an associate in the work of the gospel. The church at Antioch arose to such prominence that here for the first time the followers of Christ became known as "Christians,"—a name applied not by Jews, but by Greeks, and found only three times in the New Testament. The disciples at Antioch sent aid to the poorer saints in Judea in a time of famine; and its leaders and teachers were eminent men in the early church.

Thus far the Gentile members of the church were only those who had themselves sought admission. But now, under the guidance of the Holy Spirit and by the appointment of the elders, the two greatest leaders in the church at Antioch went forth on an evangelistic mission to other lands, seeking both

Acts 11:22, 23.

Acts 9:26, 27.

Acts 11:25, 26.

Acts 11:26.
Acts 26:28.
I Pet. 4:16.

Acts 11:27, 30.

Acts 13:1.

7. The First Missionary Journey. Acts 13 and 14.

Jews and Gentiles with the gospel. As we read the
story of this First Missionary Journey we notice
certain features in the effort, which became typical
of all the later enterprises of the Apostle Paul.

(1) Team
Work.
Acts 13:2, 15.

It was undertaken by two workers in unison, at
first "Barnabas and Saul," but soon changed to
"Paul and Barnabas," or "Paul and his company,"

Acts 13:9.

showing Saul or Paul as the leading spirit. Regarding Saul's change of name: it was customary for a
Jew to have two names, one Israelite, the other

(2) A Young
Helper.
Acts 13:5.
Acts 13:13.

used when among Gentiles. The two missionaries
took with them as helper a younger man, John
Mark, although he forsook them in the middle of

(3) Cities
Chosen.

their journey. They chose as their principal fields
of labor the large cities, visiting Salamis and Paphos
in the island of Cyprus, Antioch and Iconium in

(4) Begin-
ning in
Synagogue.

Pisidia, Lystra and Derbe in Lycaonia. Wherever
it was possible, they began their work by preaching
in the synagogue, for therein every Jew had a right
to speak, and especially an accredited rabbi, as
Paul, coming from the famous school of Gamaliel,
would be welcome. Moreover, through the synagogue they would reach not only the devout Jews,
but with them the serious, God-fearing Gentiles.

(5) Revisit-
ing the
Churches.

At Derbe, the last city visited, they were quite
near Antioch, from which they had set forth. But
instead of passing through the Cilician Gates and
returning home, they turned westward, retraced

Acts 14:23.

their steps, revisited the churches which they had
founded on their outward journey, and appointed
over them elders according to the plan of the
synagogue. We shall find these methods of work

STATUE OF THE APOSTLE, PAUL; IN THE CHURCH OF ST. PAUL
WITHOUT THE WALLS. ROME

MOSQUE OF SANCTA SOPHIA. CONSTANTINOPLE.

followed in all the after-journeys of the Apostle
Paul.

In every society or organized group of people
two types are always represented: the conservative, looking to the past, and the progressive, looking toward the future. The ultra Jewish element
in the church held that there could be no salvation
outside of Israel; hence, that all the Gentile disciples must receive circumcision and observe Jewish
regulations. The progressive teachers led by Paul
and Barnabas declared that the gospel was for Jews
and Gentiles upon the same terms of faith in Christ
without regard to the Jewish law. Between these
two parties a great controversy arose, threatening
a division in the church; and finally a council was
held in Jerusalem to consider the question of Gentile
membership, and frame a ruling for the church. It
is noteworthy that in this council not only the
apostles, but the elders, and "the whole church,"
were represented. Paul and Barnabas, with Peter
and James, the Lord's brother, took part in the
debate; and the conclusion was reached that the
law was binding upon Jews only, and not upon
Gentile believers in Christ. With this decision the
period of transition from a Jewish Christian Church
to a church for people of every race and land, was
completed; and the gospel could now go forward
on its ever-widening way.

8. The
Council at
Jerusalem,
50 A. D.
Acts 15.

Acts 15:6,
12, 22.

CHAPTER IV.

THE CHURCH AMONG THE GENTILES.

FROM THE COUNCIL AT JERUSALEM, 50 A. D., TO THE MARTYRDOM OF ST. PAUL, 68 A. D.

III. The Church Among the Gentiles, 50-68 A. D.

By the decision of the Council at Jerusalem, the church was free to enter upon a larger work for the bringing of all people, of every race, and in every land under the realm of Jesus Christ. Jewish members of the church were expected to continue in their obedience to the Jewish law, though the regulations were interpreted broadly by such leaders as St. Paul. But Gentiles could enter the Christian fold by simple faith in Christ and a righteous life, without submission to legal requirements.

1. Authorities.

For our information of the events in the twenty years following the Council we are dependent upon the Book of Acts, the letters of the Apostle Paul, and perhaps the opening verse of St. Peter's First Epistle, which may refer to lands visited by that apostle. To these authorities may be added a few traditions, seeming to be authentic, from the period immediately following the apostolic age. The field of the church is now the entire Roman Empire, consisting of all the provinces bordering upon the Mediterranean Sea, and also some lands outside

Acts 16 to 28. I Pet. 1:1.

2. Field.

(34)

its boundaries, especially upon the east. Its mem- 3. Members.
bership we shall find increasingly Gentile and
decreasingly Jewish; for as the gospel gained a
following in the heathen world the Jews drew away
from it and grew more and more bitter in their
hatred. Almost everywhere during this epoch it
was the Jews who instigated persecutions against
the Christians.

Three leaders stand prominently before the 4. Leaders.
church during those years; first, and easily chief, St. Paul.
St. Paul, the tireless traveler, the indomitable
worker, the church-founder and theologian; next
to Paul, St. Peter, whose name scarcely appears St. Peter.
upon the record, but who was recognized by St.
Paul as one of the "pillars." We are inclined to Gal. 2:9.
accept the tradition that Peter was for some time
at Rome, supervised the church in that city, and
died there as a martyr about 67 A. D. The third St. James.
of the great names in this period is that of St. James,
a younger brother of our Lord, and head of the Mark 6:3.
church in Jerusalem. He was a loyal supporter Gal. 1:19.
of the Jewish usages and recognized as a leader
among Jewish Christians, though not to the extent Acts 15:13-21
of opposing the gospel to the Gentiles. The Epistle
of James was written by this apostle. He was
slain in the Temple about 62 A. D. Thus all the
three leaders in this period, besides many of less
prominence, gave up their lives as martyrs to the
faith.

The record of these years as contained in the last 5. St. Paul's
thirteen chapters of the Book of Acts reports only Journeys.
the work of the Apostle Paul; yet there must have

been many other missionaries, for soon after the close of this epoch, churches are named in lands which Paul had never visited. Paul's first journey through some of the interior provinces of Asia Minor has been already mentioned. After the Council at Jerusalem he set out on a second missionary journey. With Silas or Silvanus as his companion, he went forth from Syrian Antioch, visited again for the third time the churches on the mainland founded on his first journey, reached the coast of the Ægean Sea at Troas, the site of ancient Troy, and crossed over into Europe, bringing the gospel to that continent. They established churches at Philippi, Thessalonica, and Berea in the province of Macedonia; a small one in the cultured city of Athens, and a strong one at Corinth, the commercial metropolis of Greece. From Corinth Paul wrote two letters to the church at Thessalonica, his earliest extant epistles. Then he sailed eastward across the Ægean Sea for a brief visit to Ephesus in Asia Minor; then over the Mediterranean to Cæsarea; went up to salute the mother church at Jerusalem; and returned to his starting-point at Syrian Antioch. In his journey of three years by land and sea he had covered more than two thousand miles, had planted the church in at least seven important cities—probably in many more—and had opened the imperial continent of Europe to the gospel.

(1) Paul's Second Journey.
Acts 15:36 to 18:22.

After a brief period of rest, Paul entered upon his third missionary journey, again from Antioch, but destined to end in Jerusalem, with himself a prisoner in the hands of the Roman government.

(2) Paul's Third Journey.
Acts 18:23 to 21:17.

His only companion in the beginning was Timothy, who had joined him on his second journey, and remained to the end his faithful helper and "son in the gospel;" but quite a number of fellow-travelers were with him before the close of this journey. He began by visiting the churches in Syria and Cilicia, doubtless including his birthplace, Tarsus; then passed over his old route, calling for the fourth time upon the churches of his first journey.* But after crossing the province of Phrygia, instead of turning northward to Troas, he went southward to Ephesus, the metropolis of Asia Minor. Here he stayed more than two years, the longest at any place in all his journeys. His ministry won great success, resulting, not only in the church at Ephesus, but also in planting the gospel throughout the province. "The seven churches of Asia" were formed either directly or indirectly by St. Paul. Following his method of revisiting his churches, from Ephesus he sailed to Macedonia, called upon the disciples in Philippi, Thessalonica, and Berea, also those in Greece. He was led to return by the same route for a final visit to those churches; sailed to Troas, and thence along the coast of Asia Minor. At Miletus, the seaport of Ephesus, he sent for the elders of that church, and gave to them a touching farewell address; then went on his voyage again to Cæsarea, and climbed up the mountains to Jerusa-

Acts 16:1-3.
Phil. 2:19-22.

Acts 19:22.
Acts 20:4.

Acts 19:10.
Rev. 1:4, 11.

Acts 20:1, 2.

Acts 20:6-12.
Acts 20:17-36.

* In tracing this journey upon the map, the student should follow the route as given by Sir William Ramsay. "Galatia," in Acts 18:23, does not refer as the older maps indicate, to a northern route through Ancyra, Pessinus, etc., but is now understood to mean South Galatia, to which belonged both Lycaonia and Pisidia. Paul's third journey followed the same course through Asia Minor as his first and second journeys.

lem. At that city his third missionary journey ended;
for while worshiping in the Temple, Paul was attacked by a Jewish mob, rescued by Roman soldiers,
and, for his own safety, placed in the castle named
after Mark Antony. The third missionary journey was
as long as the second, except for the three hundred
miles between Jerusalem and Antioch. Its greatest
outstanding results were the commanding church at
Ephesus, and two of the most important epistles of
St. Paul, one to the church at Rome setting forth the
principles of the gospel as preached by himself; and
the other, the Epistle to the Galatians, addressed
to the churches of his first journey, wherein Judaizing
teachers had perverted many of the disciples.

(3.) **Paul's
Fourth
Journey.
Acts 27
and 28.**

For more than five years after his arrest, Paul
was a prisoner, for a short time in Jerusalem, then
for three years in Cæsarea, and for at least two
years at Rome. We may look upon that perilous
voyage from Cæsarea to Rome as St. Paul's fourth
journey, for even in his bonds Paul was still a
missionary, employing every opportunity to preach
the gospel of Christ. The immediate cause of the
voyage was his appeal as a Roman citizen from the

Acts 25:9-12. trial by the procurator of Judea to the emperor's
court at Rome. His companions were Luke and

Acts 27:2. Aristarchus, who may have sailed as his servants.
There were also on board a group of convicted
criminals taken to Rome for slaughter in the gladiatorial games, soldiers to guard them, and sailors to
work the ship. We may be sure that on that long
and perilous voyage, all these fellow-travelers with
the apostle heard the gospel; also that at Sidon,

and Myra, and Crete, where the vessel paused, Paul was able to proclaim Christ. We know that he won to the faith many in the island of Melita (Malta), where, after the storm, they tarried three months. Acts 27:3, 5, 8.
Acts 28:7-11.

At last Paul arrived at Rome, the goal of his hopes for many years. A prisoner awaiting trial, he yet had his own hired house, wherein he lived, chained to a soldier. His first effort was, as always, to reach the Jews; and he held an all-day meeting with them, but finding that only a few of them were willing to accept the gospel, he turned to the Gentiles. For two years his house was a church, wherein many found Christ, especially among the soldiers of the Pretorian Guard. But his greatest work in Rome was the writing of four epistles, which are among the treasures of the church—Ephesians, Philippians, Colossians, and Philemon. There is good reason to believe that after two years in prison, Paul was acquitted and set at liberty. *Acts 28:16.* *Acts 28:17-28* *Acts 28:30, 31.* *Phil. 1:12-14.*

We might look upon Paul's three or four years of liberty as continuing his fourth missionary journey. We find hints or expectations of visits to Colosse and Miletus. If he was so near to Ephesus, as were these two places, we might be almost certain that he visited that city. He visited also the island of Crete, where he left Titus in charge of the churches; and Nicopolis on the Adriatic Sea, north of Greece. Tradition states that at this place he was arrested, and sent again to Rome, where he was martyred 68 A. D. Three epistles may belong to this period. First Timothy, Titus, and Second Timothy, his last letter, written from his prison at Rome. *Philemon 22.* *II Tim. 4:20.* *Tit. 1:5; 3:12.*

6. First Imperial Persecution, A. D. 65-68.

In the year 64 A. D. a large part of the city of Rome was destroyed in a great conflagration. It has been said that the fire was started by Nero, worst of all the Roman emperors; but this is disputed. It is certain that Nero was charged with the crime by common report. In order to clear himself, Nero declared that the Christians had set fire to the city, and began a terrible persecution.

Martyrdom of St. Paul, 68 A. D.

Thousands were tortured and put to death, among them St. Peter by crucifixion, in the year 67; and St. Paul by being beheaded, in the year 68. These dates are not certain, and the apostles may have suffered martyrdom a year, or two years, earlier. It is one of "the revenges of history," that the gardens of Nero, where multitudes of Christians were burned as "living torches," while the emperor drove his chariot among them, are now the seat of the Vatican palace, the home of the Roman Catholic pontiff, and of St. Peter's Church, the largest edifice of the Christian faith.

7. Literature of the Period.

At the time of the Council at Jerusalem, 50 A. D., none of the New Testament books had been written, and the church was dependent for its knowledge of the Saviour's life and teachings upon the memory of the earlier disciples. But before the close of this period, 68 A. D., a large part of the New Testament was in circulation, including the gospels by Matthew, Mark and Luke, the epistles of St. Paul and James, 1 Peter and perhaps II Peter, although the authorship of the last named is doubtful. It is to be remembered that the Epistle to the Hebrews was not of Pauline authorship, and was probably written after St. Paul's death.

CHAPTER V.

THE AGE OF SHADOWS.

FROM THE MARTYRDOM OF ST. PAUL, 68 A. D., TO
THE DEATH OF ST. JOHN, 100 A. D.

We name the last generation of the first century, *The Age of Shadows.* from 68 to 100 A. D., "The Age of Shadows," partly because the gloom of persecution was over the church; but more especially because of all periods in the history, it is the one about which we know the least. We have no longer the clear light of the Book of Acts to guide us; and no author of that age has filled the blank in the history. We would like to read of the later work by such helpers of St. Paul as Timothy, Apollos and Titus, but all these and St. Paul's other friends drop out of the record at his death. For fifty years after St. Paul's life a curtain hangs over the church, through which we strive vainly to look; and when at last it rises, about 120 A. D. with the writings of the earliest church-fathers, we find a church in many aspects very different from that in the days of St. Peter and St. Paul.

The fall of Jerusalem in the year 70 A. D., made *1. The Fall of Jerusalem, 70 A. D.* a great change in the relation of Christians and Jews. Among the many provinces under the rule of Rome, the only land discontented and disloyal

was Judea. The Jews, by putting their own interpretation upon their prophetic writings, believed
that they were destined to conquer and govern the
world, and having that confident expectation submitted unwillingly to the yoke of the Roman emperors.   It must be admitted also that many of the
Roman procurators or governors utterly failed to
comprehend the Jewish character, and were need-
lessly harsh in their dealings. About 66 A. D. the
Jews broke out into open rebellion, hopeless from its
very beginning, for what could one of the smallest
provinces, whose people were untrained in war,
accomplish against an empire of a hundred and
twenty millions of people, with a quarter of a
million disciplined and seasoned soldiers?   Moreover, the Jews themselves were broken into factions
which fought and slaughtered each other as fiercely
as their common enemy Rome.   Vespasian, the
leading Roman general, led a great army into
Palestine, but was called to Rome to take the
imperial throne, and left the conduct of the war to
his son Titus.   After a terrible siege, made more
terrible by starvation and civil strife within the
70 A. D.   walls, the city was taken and destroyed.   Untold
thousands of the Jews were put to death, and other
thousands were enslaved.   The Coliseum at Rome
was built by the forced labor of Jewish captives,
multitudes being literally worked to death.   The
Jewish state, after an existence of thirteen centuries
was annihilated, and has never as yet been restored.

In the fall of Jerusalem, few if any Christians
Matt. 24.   perished.   From the prophetic utterances of Christ

the Christians received warning, escaped from the doomed city, and found refuge at Pella, in the Jordan valley. But the great effect upon the church of this destruction was that it put an end forever to all relation between Judaism and Christianity. Up to this time the church had been regarded by the Roman government and by the people at large as a branch of the Jewish religion: but henceforth Jews and Christians were apart. A small section of Jewish Christians endured for two centuries, but with ever-decreasing numbers, the Ebionites, a people by themselves, scarcely recognized by the general church and despised as apostates by their own race.

About the year 90 A. D. the worthless and cruel emperor Domitian began a second imperial persecution of the Christians. Thousands of the believers were slain, especially in Rome and Italy; for this persecution, like that of Nero, was spasmodic and local, not extending throughout the empire. At this time St. John, the last of the apostles, who had been living in Ephesus, was imprisoned in the isle of Patmos, in the Ægean Sea, and there received the Revelation contained in the last book of the New Testament. Many scholars, however, assign an earlier date to this work, about 69 A. D., soon after the death of Nero. It is probable that St. John died at Ephesus about 100 A. D.

2. The Second Imperial Persecution, 90-96 A. D.

Rev. 1:9.

During this age the later books of the New Testament were written—Hebrews, perhaps II Peter, the three Epistles and Gospel of John, Jude and the Revelation. But the universal recognition of these books as inspired and canonical came later.

3. Completion of the New Testament.

4. The Condition of the Church.

It is interesting to note the state of Christianity at the close of the first century, about seventy years after the Ascension of Christ. By this date there were families which for three generations had been followers of Christ.

(1) Extent and Numbers.

At the opening of the second century the church was to be found in every land and almost every city from the Tiber to the Euphrates, from the Black Sea to Northern Africa, and some think extending as far west as Spain and Britain. Its membership included many millions. The well-known letter of Pliny to the Emperor Trajan, written about 112 A. D., states that in the provinces of Asia Minor bordering on the Black Sea the temples of the gods were almost forsaken, and the Christians were everywhere a multitude. The members were of every class, from the noblest in rank down to the slaves, who throughout the empire outnumbered the free population. But in the church, its services and its officers, the slave was treated as the equal of the noble. A slave might be a bishop, while his master was only an ordinary member.

(2) Doctrinal System.

At the end of the first century the doctrines set forth by the Apostle Paul in the Epistle to the Romans were accepted throughout the church as the standards of the faith. The teachings of St. Peter and St. John in their epistles show a complete

Acts 20:29, 30. Col. 2:18-23. I John 2:18, 19.

accord with the views of St. Paul. Heretical opinions were arising, and sects were forming, the germs of which had been noted and warned against by the apostles, but their full development came later.

Baptism was everywhere the rite of initiation into the church, mainly by immersion; although there is definite mention, 120 A. D., of baptism by pouring water upon the head, indicating that it was already a custom. The Lord's Day was generally observed, though not with strictness as a day absolutely set apart. As long as the church was mainly Jewish, the Hebrew sabbath was kept; but as it became increasingly Gentile the first day gradually took the place of the seventh day. We find before the end of St. Paul's ministry, the churches meeting on the first day of the week, and in the Revelation that day is called "The Lord's day." The Lord's Supper was universally observed. This began as a service in the home, like the Jewish Passover, out of which it was an outgrowth. But among Gentile churches the custom arose of celebrating it at a meeting of the church, as a supper to which each member brought some share of provision. St. Paul rebuked the church at Corinth for abuses that had crept into this method of observance. By the end of the century the Lord's Supper was everywhere a service held at the meeting-place of the Christians, but (probably on account of the persecutions) not in public. All except members of the church were excluded from this celebration, which was held as a "mystery." The recognition of Easter Sunday, as the anniversary of our Lord's resurrection was sanctioned and growing, but was not by this time universal.

The last survivor of the twelve apostles was St. John, dwelling at Ephesus until about 100 A. D. We read of no successors in that office; but about

(3) Institutions of the Church.
(a) Baptism.

(b) The Lord's Day.

I Cor. 16:2.
Acts 20:7.
Rev. 1:10.
(c) The Lord's Supper.
Acts 2:46.

I Cor. 11:20-30.

(d) Easter Sunday.

(4) Officers of the Church.
(a) Apostles.

120 A. D. there is mention of "apostles," who appear to have been evangelists traveling among the churches, but without authority; and evidently not highly respected, for churches are recommended to give them entertainment for three days and no longer. In the Acts and later epistles elders (presbyters) and bishops are named as though the two titles were applied interchangeably to the same persons. But by the close of the first century the tendency was growing to elevate one as bishop above his fellow-elders, leading later to an ecclesiastical system. Deacons are mentioned in St. Paul's later letters as church officers. In Romans, written about 58 A. D., Phebe of Cenchrea is called a "deaconess," and a reference in I Timothy may be to women holding that office.

(b) Bishops and Elders.
Acts 20:17, 28.
Phil. 1:1.
Titus 1:5, 7.

(c) Deacons.
Phil. 1:1.
I Tim. 3:8-13.
Rom. 16:1.
(Margin) Am Ver.
I Tim. 3:10, 11.

(5) Its Worship.

The plan of service in the Christian assemblies was derived from that in the Jewish synagogues. The Old Testament Scriptures were read, and portions of the apostolic letters, also of the gospels; the psalms of the Bible and Christian hymns were chanted; prayers, unlike those in the synagogues, were spontaneous; and addresses were freely given by the members and visiting brethren. At the close of the service frequently the Lord's Supper was partaken.

(6) Its Spiritual State.

Reading the later epistles and the Book of Revelation, we find light and shade mingled in the account of the churches. The standards of moral character were high, but the tone of spiritual life was lower than it had been in the earlier apostolic days. Yet everywhere the church was strong, aggressive, growing, and rising to dominance throughout the world of the Roman empire.

OUTLINE OF CHAPTERS VI, VII, VIII.

SECOND GENERAL PERIOD. THE PERSECUTED CHURCH.

From the Death of St. John, 100 A. D.,
To the Edict of Constantine, 313 A. D.

I. CAUSES OF THE IMPERIAL PERSECUTIONS
(CHAPTER VI).

1. Heathen Worship Hospitable; Christianity Exclusive.
2. Idol Worship Interwoven with Life.
3. Worship of the Emperor.
4. Judaism Recognized.
5. Secret Meetings of Christians.
6. Equality in the Christian Church.
7. Business Interests.

II. STAGES OF PERSECUTION (CHAPTER VI).

1. Trajan to Antoninus Pius, 96-161.
    Martyrs: (1) Simeon.   (2) Ignatius.
2. Marcus Aurelius, 161-180.
    Martyrs: (1) Polycarp.   (2) Justin Martyr.
3. Septimius Severus, 193-211.
  } Martyrs: (1) Leonidas.   (2) Perpetua and Felicitas.
4. Decius, 249-251.
5. Valerian, 254-260.
    Martyrs: Cyprian, Sextus, 258.
6. Diocletian, 303-305.   Galerius, 305-311.
    Edict of Constantine, 313.

III. FORMATION OF THE NEW TESTAMENT CANON
(CHAPTER VII).

IV. GROWTH OF ECCLESIASTICAL ORGANIZATION
(CHAPTER VII).

Causes:
1. Loss of Apostolic Authority.
2. Growth and Extent of the Church.
3. Imperial Persecutions.
4. Rise of Sects and Heresies.
5. Analogy of Imperial Government.

V. DEVELOPMENT OF DOCTRINE (CHAPTER VII).

1. School of Alexandria.
2. School of Asia Minor.
3. School of North Africa.

VI. RISE OF THE SECTS OR HERESIES (CHAPTER VIII).

1. Gnostics.
2. Ebionites.
3. Manicheans.
4. Montanists.

VII. CONDITION OF THE CHURCH (CHAPTER VIII).

1. A Purified Church.
2. A Church of Unified Teaching.
3. An Organized Church.
4. A Growing Church.

WORKS FOR FURTHER STUDY.

Cowan. Landmarks of Church History, Chaps. III, IV.
Orr. History and Literature of the Early Church, Chaps. V-X.
Selden. Story of the Christian Centuries, Chap. III.
Zenos. Compendium of Church History, Chaps. III-VI.
Rudolph Sohm. Outlines of Church History, Chaps. I, II.
Moncrief. Short History of Christian Church, Chap. II.
Epochs of Church History. The Post Apostolic Age, L. Waterman.
Fisher. History of the Christian Church, pp. 87-143.
Hurst. History of the Christian Church, Vol. I, pp. 149-409.
Schaff. History of the Christian Church, Vol. II.
James Orr. Neglected Factors in the Study of the Progress of Early Christianity.
Uhlhorn. The Conflict of Christianity with Heathenism.

CHAPTER VI.

THE IMPERIAL PERSECUTIONS.

Second
Period.
The
Persecuted
Church,
100-313 A. D.

FROM THE DEATH OF ST. JOHN, 100 A. D., TO THE
EDICT OF CONSTANTINE, 313 A. D.

The most prominent fact in the history of the
church through the second and third centuries is
the persecution of Christianity by the Roman
emperors. While this condition was not continuous, it was often repeated for years at a time, and
liable to break forth at any moment in terrible
forms. It lasted in the fourth century until 313
A. D., when the Edict of Constantine, the first
Christian emperor, ended all attempts to destroy
the Church of Christ. The fact is remarkable that
during this period some of the wisest and best of the
emperors were the most active in the persecution of
Christianity, while some of the worst emperors were
lax in their opposition or remitted it altogether.
Before narrating the history, let us investigate
some of the motives that impelled a government, in
the main just and seeking the welfare of its citizens,
to attempt, and continue for two hundred years, the
extirpation of a body as upright, as law-abiding,
and as desirable as the Christians. A number of
causes may be named for the antagonism of the
emperors to Christianity.

The Imperial Persecutions.

1. Causes of Persecution.

(49)

1. Heathen Worship Hospitable to New Gods.

Heathenism was hospitable to new forms and objects of worship, while Christianity was exclusive. Where gods were already counted by the hundred, even by the thousand, one more god would make no difference. When the people of a city or a province desired to promote trade or immigration, they would build temples to the deities worshiped in other lands, in order that their citizens could have a place for worship. Thus in Pompeii we find a temple to Isis, an Egyptian goddess, erected to increase the commerce of Pompeii with Egypt, and make Egyptian traders at home. But on the other hand, Christianity opposed all worship except to its own God. One emperor wished to place a statue of Christ in the Pantheon, a building at Rome, still standing, where all the important gods were worshiped. But the Christians rejected the offer with scorn. They would not have their Christ recognized merely as *one* of many deities.

2. Idol Worship Interwoven with Life.

Idol worship was interwoven with life in every department. Images stood in every house to receive adoration; libations were poured out to the gods at every festival; with every civic or provincial ceremony the images were worshiped. In such forms the Christians would take no part. Hence they were regarded by the unthinking as unsocial and morose, as atheists, having no gods, and as haters of their fellow-men. From such an unfavorable estimate by people in general, it was but a step to persecution.

3. Emperor Worship.

One form of idolatry was held as a test of loyalty, the worship of the emperor. In some prominent place of every city stood a statue of the reigning

emperor; and before this image incense was offered
as to a god.   It may be that in one of St. Paul's   II Thess.
earliest epistles there is a guarded reference to this   2:3, 4.
form of idolatry.   This worship the Christians
refused to render, simple as it was to drop a handful
of incense upon the altar; and because they sang
hymns of praise and gave worship to "another   Acts 17:7.
King, one Jesus," they were looked upon by the
multitude as disloyal and plotters of a revolution.

In the first generation of the Christians, they   4. Judaism
were regarded as somehow connected with the Jews,   Recognized.
and Judaism was recognized by the government as
a permitted religion, although the Jews lived apart
from the idolatrous customs, and would not even
eat food from the idol-feasts.   This supposed rela-
tionship for a time preserved the Christians from
persecution. But after the destruction of Jerusalem,
in 70 A. D., Christianity stood alone with no laws to
protect its followers from the hatred of their enemies.

The secret meetings of Christians aroused sus-   5. Secret
picion.   They met either before sunrise or at night,   Meetings.
often in caves or catacombs underground; and
false reports went abroad of lascivious or murderous
rites performed among them.   Moreover, the autocratic government of the empire was jealous of all
secret cults or societies, fearing disloyal aims.   The
celebration of the Lord's Supper, from which out-
siders were excluded, was often made a ground for
accusation and persecution.

Christianity looked upon all men as equal.   It   6. Equality in
made no distinctions in its membership and its ser-   the Church.
vices; a slave might be chosen as bishop in the

church. This was abhorrent to the minds of the nobles, to the philosophic, and to the ruling classes. The Christians were regarded as "levellers," anarchists, and subverters of the social order; hence as enemies of the state.

7. Business Interests.

Acts 19.

Incidentally, business interests often promoted or excited the persecuting spirit. Just as St. Paul at Ephesus was thrown into danger of death through the riot incited by Demetrius the silversmith, often the rulers were influenced to persecute the Christians by people whose financial interests were affected by the progress of the church; e. g. the priests and lay-servants of the idol temples, image makers, sculptors, architects of the temples, and others whose living depended upon the heathen worship. It was not difficult to raise the cry, "The Christians to the lions!" when men found their craft in danger, or covetous officials longed for the property of wealthy Christians.

II. Stages of Persecution.

During all the second and third century, and especially in the opening years of the fourth century, to the year 313 A. D., the Christian religion was forbidden and its votaries were outlawed. Yet most of the time the sword of persecution was sheathed, and the disciples were scarcely interrupted in their religious observances. But even during those periods of comparative rest they were at any time liable to sudden danger, whenever a provincial governor saw fit to execute the edicts, or when some prominent Christian was open and bold in his testimony. There were, however, several periods, of shorter or longer duration, when throughout the empire, the church was exposed to the fiercest persecution. We have noticed the persecutions in the first century, by Nero (66–68) and Domitian (90–95). These were simply outbreaks of frenzy and hate, with no reason except the rage of a tyrant, spasmodic, occasional and not long continued. But from 110 to 313 A. D. the church was subjected to a systematic, relentless, empire-wide series of attempts by the government to crush the ever-growing faith.

From the reign of Trajan to that of Antoninus Pius (96–161 A. D.) Christianity was not recognized, yet was not severely persecuted. Under the four emperors, Nerva, Trajan, Hadrian and Antoninus Pius (who with the next in succession, Marcus Aurelius, were known as "the five good emperors"), no Christians could be arrested without a definite and proven complaint, and the spirit of the age was to ignore the Christian religion. Yet when charges were made and Christians refused to recant, the rulers were compelled, even unwillingly, to enforce the law and put them to death. Prominent martyrs to the faith during those reigns were:

1. Trajan to Antoninus Pius, 96–161 A. D.

Simeon (or Simon, Mark 6:3), the successor of St. James as head or bishop of the church in Jerusalem, and like him was also a brother of our Lord; said to have attained the age of one hundred and twenty years. He was crucified by order of the Roman governor of Palestine in 107 A. D. during the reign of Trajan.

Martyrs.
(1) Simeon, 107 A. D.

Ignatius, bishop of Antioch in Syria, was more than willing to be a martyr, and on his way to Rome

(2) Ignatius, 110 A. D.

wrote letters to the churches, hoping that he might not lose the honor of dying for his Lord.   He was thrown to wild beasts in the Roman amphitheatre, 108 or 110 A. D.   Although the persecution during these reigns was less severe than that falling upon the church soon afterward, there were many martyrs beside these two distinguished men.

2. Marcus Aurelius, 161-180 A. D.   The very best of the Roman emperors, and one of the highest type of ethical writers, was Marcus Aurelius, who reigned 161 to 180 A. D.   His equestrian statue still stands before the site of the ancient Capitol in Rome.   Yet this good man and just ruler was a bitter persecutor of the Christians.   He sought to restore the old simplicity of Roman life, and with it the ancient religion; and opposed the Christians as innovators.   Many thousands of the believers in Christ were beheaded or devoured by wild beasts in the arena.   Among the multitude of the martyrs during those years we mention only two.

Martyrs. (1) Polycarp. 155 A. D.   Polycarp, bishop of Smyrna in Asia Minor, died in 155 A. D.   When brought before the governor and commanded to curse the name of Jesus Christ, he answered, "Eighty and six years have I served him, and he has done me nothing but good; and how could I curse him, my Lord and Saviour!"   He was burned to death.

(2) Justin, 166 A. D.   Justin Martyr had been a philosopher, and continued teaching after his acceptance of Christianity. He was one of the ablest men of his time, and a foremost defender of the faith.   His books, still extant, give much valuable information concerning the church in the middle of the second century. His martyrdom took place at Rome in 166 A. D.

After the death of Marcus Aurelius, 180 A. D., a period of confusion followed, with weak and worthless emperors, who were too busy with civil wars or their own pleasures to pay much attention to the Christians. But Septimius Severus began in the year 202 a fierce persecution which lasted until his death in 211 A. D. Severus was morbid and melancholy in nature, and a strong disciplinarian, striving vainly to restore the decaying religions of other days. Everywhere persecution raged against the church, but it was the most severe in Egypt and North Africa. In Alexandria, Leonidas, the father of the great theologian Origen was beheaded. A noble lady in Carthage, Perpetua, with her faithful slave Felicitas, was torn in pieces by wild beasts 203 A. D. So bitter was the spirit of the emperor, Septimius Severus, that he was regarded by many Christian writers as the Antichrist.

3. Septimius Severus, 202-211 A. D.

Martyrs.
(1) Leonidas, 202 A. D.
(2) Perpetua and Felicitas, 203 A. D.

Under the numerous emperors who followed in rapid succession, the church was left unnoticed for forty years. The emperor, Caracalla (211–217 A. D.), conferred citizenship upon every person not a slave throughout the empire; incidentally a benefit to the Christians, as they could no longer be crucified or thrown to wild beasts, unless they were slaves. But with the reign of Decius (249–251) fierce persecution broke out anew, though fortunately his reign was very short, and the slaughter of Christians ended for a time with his death.

I John 2:18, 22

4. Decius, 249-251 A. D.

5. Valerian,
257 A. D.
Martyrs.
Cyprian.

More than fifty years of comparative rest followed the death of Decius, although there came at times brief periods of persecution, in one of which, under Valerian, in 257 A. D., the celebrated Cyprian, bishop of Carthage, one of the great writers and church-leaders of the period, was put to death; also the Roman Bishop Sextus.

Sextus,
258 A. D.

6. Diocletian.
303-310 A. D.

The last, most systematic and most terrible persecution of all the series took place in the reign of Diocletian and his successors, from 303 to 310 A. D. In a series of edicts it was ordered that every copy of the Bible should be burned; that all churches —which had arisen throughout the empire during the half-century of comparative rest from persecution—should be torn down; that all who would not renounce the Christian religion should lose their citizenship and be outside the protection of law. In some places the Christians were assembled in their churches, which were set on fire and burned with all the worshipers within their walls. It is said that the emperor, Diocletian, erected a pillar inscribed, "In honor of the extirpation of the Christian superstition"*—yet within twenty-five years Christianity became the official religion of the emperor, the court, and the empire. With the forced labor of enslaved Christians the immense Baths of Diocletian were erected at Rome. But twelve centuries after Diocletian's time, a part of his building was transformed by Michael Angelo into the Church of Santa Maria degli Angeli, conse-

---

* This statement, though made by many historians, rests upon uncertain evidence, and may not be authentic.

crated in 1561 A. D. and still in use for Christian worship.   Diocletian abdicated the imperial throne in 305 A. D., but his subordinates and successors, Galerius and Constantius, continued the persecution for six years.   Constantine, the son of Constantius, as co-emperor, who was not at that time a professing Christian, issued his memorable Edict of Toleration in 313 A. D.   By this law Christianity was sanctioned, its worship was made lawful, and all persecution ceased, not to be renewed while the Roman Empire endured.

CHAPTER VII.

THE PERSECUTED CHURCH.

PART TWO.

FORMATION OF THE NEW TESTAMENT CANON.
GROWTH OF ECCLESIASTICAL ORGANIZA-
TION. DEVELOPMENT OF DOCTRINE.

While the great outstanding fact in the history of
the church throughout the second and third centuries was the imperial persecutions, at the same
time great developments were taking place in the
condition, organization, and life of the Christian
community. Some of these we will now consider.

**III. Forma-
tion of
the New
Testament
Canon.**
We have already seen that the New Testament
writings were finished soon after the beginning of
the second century, perhaps as early as 110 A. D.
But the establishment of these books, and these
only, as the canon or rule of faith, possessing a
divine authority, was not immediate. Not all these
books were accepted everywhere as inspired Scripture. Some of them, notably Hebrews, James, II
Peter and Revelation, were accepted in the East,
but rejected for many years in the West. On the
other hand some books not now considered as
belonging to the Bible were also accepted and read
in the East, such as the Shepherd of Hermas, the
Epistle of Barnabas, the Teaching of the Twelve

Apostles, and the Apocalypse of Peter. By slow degrees the New Testament books as we now have them gradually took the rank of Scripture, and the other books as gradually dropped out of use in the churches. The councils that were held from time to time did not *choose* the books to form the canon; they ratified the choice already made among the churches. No precise date can be given for the full recognition of the New Testament as it is at present, but it cannot be placed earlier than 300 A. D. Any one who will read the volume of "The New Testament Apocrypha," and compare its contents with our New Testament, will see at once why these books were finally rejected from the canon.

While the original apostles were living, the universal reverence for them as the chosen companions of Christ, the founders of the church, and men endowed with special divine inspiration, made them the unquestioned leaders of the church, and its rulers, as far as rule was needed. When St. Luke wrote the Book of Acts and St. Paul wrote to the Philippians and to Timothy, the titles "bishops" and "elders" (presbyters) were applied freely to the same officials. But sixty years later, about 125 A. D., we find that bishops were everywhere ruling over the church, each commanding his own diocese, with presbyters and deacons under his authority. About 50 A. D. the Council at Jerusalem was composed of "the apostles and elders," and expressed the voice of the whole church, both ministers (if there were such, which is doubtful) and laymen. But during the period of the persecutions, certainly

IV. Growth of Ecclesiastical Organization.

Acts 15.

after 150 A. D., the councils were held and rules were made by bishops only. The episcopal form of government became dominant and universal. There is no history of the time to tell us the steps leading to this change in organization, but it is not difficult to find its causes.

Causes of Change.
1. Loss of the Apostles.

The loss of apostolic authority made a choice of new leaders necessary. The great founders of the church, Peter and Paul, James, the Lord's brother, and John, the last of the apostles—passed away leaving no men of their own ability to succeed them. For fifty or sixty years after the death of St. Peter and St. Paul, the history of the church is a blank. What may have been accomplished under such men as Timothy, Titus, and Apollos, we know not; but a generation afterward new names appear as bishops with authority over their several dioceses.

2. Growth of the Church.

The growth and extent of the church made organization and discipline necessary. While the churches were limited to lands where they could receive occasional visits from apostles, few officers were needed. But when the church became as wide as the empire, and even wider, reaching to Parthia and the borders of India, embracing many lands and races, the need of headship for its various sections was realized.

3. Persecutions.

The persecutions—a common danger—drew the churches together, and exercised an influence toward union and government. When at any time the powers of the state might be arrayed against the church, the need of efficient leadership was realized; the leaders arose for the occasion; and the need

lasting through seven generations, made the form of
rule permanent.

The rise of sects and heresies in the church made **4. Heretical Sects.**
some standards of faith and some authority to
enforce them absolutely necessary. We shall notice
in this chapter some of the doctrinal divisions which
threatened the very existence of the church; and
we shall see how the controversies over them
awakened an imperative demand for discipline to
deal with heretics and insure the unity of the faith.

When we enquire why this particular form of **5. Analogy with Empire.**
government was adopted, a government from above
by bishops, in preference to one by the ministry as
equals, we find that the analogy of the imperial
government furnished a plan naturally followed in
the development of the church. Christianity arose,
not in a republic where citizens chose their own
rulers, but in an empire ruled by authority. Hence
as some government was necessary for the church,
everywhere a form somewhat autocratic arose, the
rule by bishops, to which the church willingly
submitted, being accustomed to the same rule in
the state. It is, however, a noteworthy fact that
during the entire period under consideration, no
bishop claimed universal rule, a bishop above the
bishops, as did the bishop of Rome later.

Another marked feature of this period was the **V. Develop-**
development of doctrine. In the apostolic age faith **ment of Doctrine.**
was of the heart, a personal surrender of the will to
Christ as Lord and King, a life in accordance with
his example, and as a result the indwelling of his
Spirit. But in the period which we are now study-

ing, faith had gradually come to be of the mind, an intellectual faith, believing in a hard and fast system of doctrine. Emphasis was laid on correct belief, rather than on the inner, spiritual life. The standards of Christian character were still high, and the church embraced many saints enriched by the Holy Spirit; but doctrine was becoming more and more the test of Christianity. "The Apostles' Creed," the earliest and the simplest statement of Christian belief, was composed during this period. Three great schools of theology arose, at Alexandria, in Asia Minor, and in North Africa. These schools were established for the instruction of those who, from heathen homes, had taken the vows of the Christian faith; but they soon developed into centers of investigation into the doctrines of the church. With all of these schools great teachers were associated.

Schools of Theology.

1. School of Alexandria, 180 A. D. Pantaenus. Clement. Origen.

The school at Alexandria was founded about 180 A. D. by Pantaenus, who had been a stoic philosopher, but as a Christian was eminent for fervency of spirit and eloquence in oral teaching. Only brief fragments of his writings have survived. He was succeeded by Clement of Alexandria (living about 150–215 A. D.), several of whose books, mostly in defense of Christianity against paganism, are still extant. But the greatest of the Alexandrian school, and the ablest thinker and expositor of all the period, was Origen (185–254 A. D.), who taught and wrote on many subjects, displaying vast learning and intellectual power.

2. School of Asia Minor. Irenaeus.

The school of Asia Minor was not located in any one center, but consisted of a group of theological

teachers and writers.   Its greatest representative
was Irenaeus, who "combined the zeal of the evan-
gelist with the skill of the finished writer."*   In
his later life he removed to Gaul (France), became a
bishop, and about 200 A. D. died as a martyr.

The school in North Africa was at Carthage, and
through a series of able writers and theologians, did
more than either of the other schools to shape the
theological thought of Europe.   The two greatest
names in this school were those of the brilliant and
ardent Tertullian (160–220 A. D.) and the more
conservative but masterful Bishop Cyprian, who
died as a martyr in the Decian persecution, 258 A. D.

3. School of
North Africa.
Tertullian.
Cyprian.

The writings of these Christian scholars, as well as
of many others associated with them and inspired by
them, have been of priceless value, as our source of
first-hand information concerning the church, its life,
its doctrines, and its relation to the heathen world
around it, during the centuries of persecution.

* Bishop Hurst's Church History,

CHAPTER VIII.

THE PERSECUTED CHURCH, 100–313 A. D.

PART THREE.

RISE OF THE SECTS OR HERESIES. CONDITION OF THE CHURCH.

VI. Rise of Sects or Heresies. Side by side with the development of theological doctrine was the rise of the sects, or as they were called, the heresies in the Christian church. As long as the church was Jewish in its membership, and even afterward while it was controlled by practical men of the Jewish type, such men as St. Peter and St. Paul, there was only a slight tendency toward abstract and speculative thinking. But when the church found its largest constituency among the Greeks, and especially the mystical, unbalanced Greeks of Asia Minor, all sorts of strange opinions and theories arose, and grew to power in the church. The Christians of the second and third centuries battled not only against a persecuting heathen world, but also against heresies and corrupt doctrines within their own fold. We can notice only a few of the most important among the sects of that period.

1. Gnostics. The Gnostics (Greek *gnosis*, "knowledge") are not easy to define, because so varied in their doctrines in different localities and at different periods.

They arose in Asia Minor—that hot-bed of wild imaginations—and were a grafting of Christianity upon paganism. They believed that out of the supreme God emanated a large number of inferior deities, some beneficent, others malignant; and through these the world with its mingled good and evil, was created; that in Christ as one of these "emanations," the divine nature was for a time indwelling; and they interpreted the Scriptures in an allegorical manner, making every statement mean whatever the interpreter saw fit. They flourished throughout the second century, and disappeared with it.

The Ebionites (from a Hebrew word meaning "poor") were Jewish Christians who insisted that the Jewish laws and customs should be observed. They rejected the writings of St. Paul, because these recognized Gentiles as Christians. They were despised by the Jews as apostates, and found little sympathy from the Gentile Christians, who, after 70 A. D., were dominant in the church. The Ebionites gradually dwindled away in the second century. **2. Ebionites.**

The Manichees or Manicheans, of Persian origin, were named from their founder Mani, who was put to death 276 A. D. by the Persian government. His teachings were that the universe is two kingdoms, one of light and one of darkness, each striving for mastery in nature and in man. They rejected Jesus, but believed in a "celestial Christ." They were severe in asceticism, and abjured marriages; were persecuted by both the heathen and the Christian emperors. Augustine, the greatest theo- **3. Manicheans.**

logian of the church, was a Manichean before his conversion.

4. Montanists. The Montanists, named from their founder Montanus, should scarcely be classed among the heretical sects, though their teachings were condemned by the church. They were Puritans, claiming to return to the simplicity of the primitive Christians. They believed in the priesthood of all true believers, and not in orders of the ministry; sought for a strict discipline in the church; held to prophetic gifts as the privilege of disciples, and had many prophets and prophetesses in their membership. Tertullian, one of the greatest among the early fathers, embraced their views, and wrote in their defense. In modern times John Wesley gave approval to Montanus and most of his teachings; and Harnack, an eminent modern scholar, has also endorsed them.

With regard to these sects and so-called heresies, one difficulty in understanding them arises from the fact that (except with the Montanists, and even there in large measure), their own writings have perished; and we are dependent for our views upon those who wrote against them, and were undoubtedly prejudiced. Suppose for example, that the Methodists as a denomination had passed out of existence with all their literature; and a thousand years afterward, scholars should attempt to ascertain their teachings out of the books and pamphlets written against John Wesley in the eighteenth century, what wrong conclusions would be reached, and what a distorted portrait of Methodism would be presented!

Let us now endeavor to ascertain the condition of the church during the ages of persecution, and especially at its close, about 313 A. D. VII. Condition of the Church.

One effect of the trials through which the Christians of that period passed was a purified church. The persecutions kept away all who were not sincere in their profession; none joined the church for wordly gain or popularity. The half-hearted and the weak left it; only those became the open followers of Christ who were willing to be faithful unto death. Persecution sifted the church, drove away the chaff and left the wheat in its membership. 1. A Purified Church.

It was upon the whole a church of unified teaching. Here was a body of many millions of people, extended over many lands, embracing many races, speaking many languages, yet holding to one faith. The various sects arose, flourished, and by degrees perished; the controversies brought out the truth, and even many of the heresies left behind them some truths which enriched the church's deposit. Despite sects and schisms, the Christianity of the empire and of the lands around it was one in its doctrine, its system and its spirit. 2. Unified Teaching.

It was a thoroughly organized church. We have seen how the system of organization grew up from the loosely co-ordinated elements in the apostolic age. By the third century the church was everywhere divided into dioceses, with bishops holding the reins of government in firm hands. The church was an army, disciplined, united, under able leadership. In the empire of Rome, outwardly well organized, but inwardly decaying, was another 3. An Organized Church.

empire of abounding life and advancing power, the Christian church.

4. A Growing Church.   It was a growing church.   In spite of the persecutions, perhaps to some extent on account of them, the church was growing with marvelous rapidity. At the close of the persecuting period the church was numerous enough to constitute the most powerful institution in the empire.   Gibbon, the historian of this period, estimated the Christians at the end of the persecutions at less than one-tenth of the population, and many writers since have accepted his statements.   But recently the whole subject has been carefully investigated, and the conclusion of present-day scholarship is that the members of the church, and its adherents, numbered half of the one hundred and twenty millions under the dominion of Rome.   One remarkable line of evidence has been found in the catacombs of Rome, underground quarries of vast extent, which for two centuries became the hiding-places, the meeting-places, and the burial-places of the believers, wherein the graves of Christians, as shown by the inscriptions and symbols upon them, are estimated by some to number seven million, and by no explorers less than two million.   Perhaps four million in seven generations would be a fair conclusion.   Add to these millions more not buried in the catacombs; and then consider how vast must have been the aggregate in the Roman empire.

OUTLINE OF CHAPTERS IX, X, XI.

THIRD GENERAL PERIOD. THE IMPERIAL CHURCH.

From the Edict of Constantine, 313 A. D.,
To the Fall of Rome, 476 A. D.

I. THE VICTORY OF CHRISTIANITY (CHAPTER IX).

1. Constantine, the First Christian Emperor.
2. Good Results to the Church.
    (1) Persecution Ended.
    (2) Churches Restored.
    (3) Official Sacrifices Ceased.
    (4) Temples Consecrated as Churches.
    (5) Endowment of Churches.
    (6) Privileges Bestowed on the Clergy.
    (7) Sunday Proclaimed as Day of Rest.
3. Some Good Results to the State.
    (1) Crucifixion Abolished.
    (2) Infanticide Repressed.
    (3) Slavery Modified.
    (4) Gladiatorial Games Suppressed.
4. Some Evil Results of the Christian Victory.
    (1) Everybody in the Church.
    (2) Pagan Usages Crept into the Church.
    (3) The Church Became Worldly.
    (4) Evils of Church United with State.

II. THE FOUNDING OF CONSTANTINOPLE (CHAPTER X).

1. The Need of a New Capital.
2. Its Location.
3. The Capital and the Church.
4. The Church of Sancta Sophia.

III. THE DIVISION OF THE EMPIRE (CHAPTER X).

IV. THE SUPPRESSION OF HEATHENISM (CHAPTER X).

1. Constantine Tolerant.
2. His Successors Intolerant.
    (1) Endowments of Temples Confiscated
    (2) Heathen Rites Interdicted.
    (3) Many Temples Demolished.
    (4) Anti-Christian Writing, Destroyed.
    (5) Idol-worship Prohibited.

V. THE CONTROVERSIES AND THE COUNCILS
(CHAPTER X).

1. Arianism—Doctrine of the Trinity.
2. Apollinarian Heresy—Nature of Christ.
3. Pelagianism—Sin and Salvation.

VI. THE RISE OF MONASTICISM (CHAPTER X).

1. Its Origin.
2. Its Founder.
3. Pillar Saints.
4. Monasticism in Europe.

VII. GROWTH OF POWER IN THE ROMAN CHURCH
(CHAPTER XI)

Causes:
 1. The Analogy of Imperial Rule.
 2. Assertion of Apostolic Sanction.
 3. The Character of the Roman Church.
    (1) The Bishops of Rome.
    (2) The Church at Rome.
 4. The Transfer of the Capital.

VIII. THE DOWNFALL OF WESTERN ROMAN EMPIRE
(CHAPTER XI).

1. Causes of Its Overthrow.
    (1) Riches of the Empire Coveted.
    (2) Romans Unused to War.
    (3) The Empire Weakened by Civil Wars.
    (4) Movement of Asiatic Tribes.
2. The Invading Tribes.
    (1) Visigoths, 376.
    (2) Vandals, 406.
    (3) Burgundians, 414.
    (4) Franks, 420.
    (5) Saxons and Angles, 440.
    (6) Huns, 450.
3. The Fall of Rome, 476 A. D.
4. The Church and the Barbarians.

IX. LEADERS IN THE PERIOD (CHAPTER XI).

1. Athanasius, 293-373 A. D.
2. Ambrose of Milan, 340-397 A. D.
3. John Chrysostom, 345-407 A. D.
4. Jerome, 340-420 A. D.
5. Augustine, 354-430 A. D.

WORKS FOR FURTHER STUDY.

Cowan. Landmarks of Church History, Chaps. V-IX.
Orr. History and Literature of the Early Church, Chap. XI.
Selden. Story of the Christian Centuries, pp. 73-95.
Zenos. Compendium of Church History, Chaps. VII-X.
Sohm. Outlines of Church History, Chap. III.
Moncrief. Short History of the Christian Church, Chaps. II, III.
Epochs of Church History. W.P.Du Bose. The Ecumenical Councils.
Fisher. History of the Christian Church, pp. 87-143.
Hurst. History of the Christian Church, Vol. I, pp. 410-464.
Schaff. History of the Christian Church, Vol. III.
Charles Kingsley. Hypatia. (Fiction.)

CHAPTER IX.

THE IMPERIAL CHURCH.

THIRD GENERAL PERIOD.

FROM THE EDICT OF CONSTANTINE, 313 A. D., TO
THE FALL OF ROME, 476 A. D. THE
VICTORY OF CHRISTIANITY.

In the period upon which we are now entering, the most striking fact, and the most potent for good and also for evil, was the victory of Christianity. In the year 305 A. D. when Diocletian abdicated the imperial throne, the Christian religion was sternly prohibited, its profession was punished with torture and death, and against it all the power of the state was called into exercise. Less than twenty years afterward, in 324 A. D., Christianity was recognized as the official religion of the Roman empire, and a Christian emperor held supreme authority, with a court of professed Christians around him. It seemed but a single step from facing lions in the amphitheatre to a place beside the throne of the world!

I. The Victory of Christianity.

Soon after the abdication of Diocletian, in 305 A. D., four aspirants after the imperial crown were at war. The two most powerful rivals were Maxentius and Constantine, whose armies met in battle

1. The First Christian Emperor, 312-337.

(73)

Battle of
the Milvian
Bridge,
312 A. D.

at the Milvian Bridge over the Tiber, ten miles from Rome, 312 A. D.   Maxentius represented the old heathen persecuting element; Constantine was friendly to the Christians, although at that time not a professed believer.   He claimed to have seen

Sign of the
Cross.

in the sky a shining cross bearing the motto, "Hoc Signo Vinces"—"By this sign thou shalt conquer," and afterward adopted it as the standard of his army.   The victory was with Constantine, and Maxentius was drowned in the river.   Soon afterward, in 313 A. D., Constantine promulgated his

Edict of
Toleration.

famous Edict of Toleration, which officially put an end to the persecutions.   Not until 323 A. D. did Constantine become sole emperor, and then Chris-

Constantine's
Character.

tianity was enthroned.   Constantine's personal character was not perfect.   Though generally just he was occasionally cruel and tyrannical.   It has been said that "the reality of his Christianity was better than its quality."   He delayed his baptism until just before his death, in the prevalent opinion of his time that baptism washed away all sins previously committed.   He was certainly a wise politician, if not a great Christian; for he had the insight to ally himself with the movement which held the future of his empire.

2. Good
Results to
the Church.

From this sudden change of relations between the empire and the church, world-wide and far-reaching results followed; some of them good, some of them evil, both to the church and the state.   We can readily see wherein the new attitude of the government brought benefits to the cause of Christianity.

All persecution of the Christians ceased at once and forever. For more than two hundred years, at no time had a Christian been safe from accusation and death, and at many periods, as we have seen, all had been in imminent danger. But from the publication of Constantine's Edict, in 313 A. D., until the Roman empire ended, the sword of persecution was not merely sheathed; it was buried.

(1) Persecution Ended.

The church buildings were restored and re-opened everywhere. In the apostolic period, meetings had been held in private houses or in hired halls. Afterward, during times of cessation in the persecutions, church buildings began to arise. In the last persecution, that under Diocletian, many of these buildings were destroyed and others were seized by the authorities. All left standing were now restored, and the cities reimbursed the societies for those which had been demolished. From this time the Christians were free to build churches; and edifices began to arise everywhere. In their plan, they followed the form and took the name of the Roman *basilica* or court-room: a rectangle divided into aisles by rows of pillars, having at one end a semicircular platform with seats for the clergy. Constantine set the example of building large churches in Jerusalem, Bethlehem, and his new capital, Constantinople. It was two generations after Constantine when images began to appear in the churches; the early Christians having a horror of all that might lead to idolatry.

(2) Churches Restored.
Acts 18:7.
Col. 4:15.
Philem. 1:2.
Acts 19:9.

Although the heathen worship was still tolerated, the official sacrifices ceased. The fact that so radi-

(3) Official Sacrifices Ceased.

cal a change from universal customs, interwoven with every social and civic celebration, could be so speedily accomplished, shows that the heathen observances had long been mere formalities, and no longer expressed the belief of intelligent people.

(4) Temples Consecrated. In many places the temples were consecrated as churches. This was especially the case in cities; while in remote country places heathen beliefs and worship lingered for generations. The word "pagan" originally meant "country-dweller;" but it came to mean, and still means "heathen."

(5) Endowment of Churches. Throughout the empire, the temples of the gods had been supported mainly from the public treasury. These endowments were now bestowed upon the churches and the clergy. At first gradually, but soon more generally and more liberally, the public funds were enriching the church, and the bishops, priests, and other officials in the Christian worship were receiving their support from the state, a welcome endowment to the church, but eventually of questionable benefit.

(6) Privileges of the Clergy. Many privileges were bestowed upon the clergy, not all by imperial enactment, but by custom which soon became law. Public duties obligatory upon all citizens were no longer required of the clergy; they were set free from taxes; all accusations against clergymen were tried before ecclesiastical courts. The ministers of the church soon became a privileged class, above the law of the land. This, also, while an immediate benefit, developed into an evil, both to the state and the church.

The first day of the week was proclaimed as a day of rest and of worship, and its observance soon became general throughout the empire. In 321 A. D. Constantine forbade the courts to be held on Sunday, except for the purpose of giving freedom to slaves; and on that day soldiers were commanded to omit their daily military exercises. But the public games were continued on Sunday, tending to make it more a holiday than a holy-day. (7) Observance of Sunday.

From the recognition of Christianity as the favored religion some good results came to the people, as well as to the church. The spirit of the new religion was infused into many of the ordinances enacted by Constantine and his immediate successors. 3. Good Results of the State.

Crucifixion was abolished. This had been a common form of execution for criminals, except such as were Roman citizens, who alone had the right to be beheaded when condemned to death. But the cross, with Christians a sacred emblem, was soon adopted by Constantine as the standard of his army, and was forbidden as a method of inflicting death. (1) Crucifixion Abolished.

Infanticide was discouraged and repressed. Through all the former history of Rome and its provinces any infant unwelcome to its father had been either smothered or "exposed," that is, thrown out to die. Some people made a business of gathering abandoned infants, bringing them up, and selling them as slaves. The influence of Christianity imparted a sacredness to human life, even in the youngest child; and caused the widespread (2) Infanticide Repressed.

evil of infanticide to disappear throughout the empire.

(3) Slavery Modified. Through all the history of the Roman republic and of the empire until Christianity became dominant, more than half of the population were slaves, without the slightest protection of law. A man could kill his slaves, if he had the whim to do so. Under one of the early emperors, a wealthy Roman was murdered by one of his slaves, and by law all the three hundred slaves in his household were put to death, regardless of their sex or age, their guilt or innocence. But with Christianity in control, the treatment of slaves at once became more humane; legal rights were given them never possessed before. They could bring accusation of cruel treatment against masters; and emancipation was sanctioned and encouraged. Thus everywhere the condition of slaves was ameliorated and slavery was gradually abolished.

(4) Gladiatorial Games Suppressed. The gladiatorial games were interdicted. This law was enforced in Constantine's new capital, where the Hippodrome was never defiled by men slaughtering each other for the pleasure of the spectators; but the combats lingered in the Roman amphitheatre until 404 A. D., when the monk Telemachus leaped into the arena and endeavored to part the gladiators. He was slain, but from that time the killing of men for the enjoyment of a crowd ceased.

4. Evil Results of the Christian Victory. But while the triumph of Christianity resulted in much that was good, inevitably the alliance of the state and the church also brought in its train many evils. The ceasing of persecution was a blessing, but the establishment of Christianity as the state religion became a curse.

Everybody sought membership in the church, and nearly everybody was received. Both good and bad, sincere seekers after God and hypocritical seekers after gain, rushed into the communion. Ambitious, worldly, unscrupulous men sought office in the church for social and political influence. The moral tone of Christianity in power was far below that which had marked the same people under persecution. *(1) Everybody in the Church.*

The services of worship increased in splendor, but were less spiritual and hearty than those of former times. The forms and ceremonies of paganism gradually crept into the worship. Some of the old heathen feasts became church festivals with change of name and of worship. About 405 A. D. images of saints and martyrs began to appear in the churches, at first as memorials, then in succession revered, adored, and worshiped. The adoration of the Virgin Mary was substituted for the worship of Venus and Diana; the Lord's Supper became a sacrifice in place of a memorial; and the elder evolved from a preacher into a priest. *(2) Pagan Usages.*

As a result of the church sitting in power, we do not see Christianity transforming the world to its own ideal, but the world dominating the church. The humility and saintliness of an earlier age was succeeded by ambition, pride, and arrogance, among churchmen. There were still many Christians of pure spirit, like Monica the mother of Augustine, *(3) A Worldly Church.*

and faithful ministers, such as Jerome and John Chrysostom; but the tide of worldliness swept uncontrolled over many professed disciples of their lowly Lord.

(4) Evils from Church United with State. If Christianity could have been allowed to develop normally without state-control, and the state could have continued free from the dictation of the church, both state and church would have been the better by dwelling apart. But the church and the state became one when Christianity was adopted as the religion of the empire, and out of the unnatural union arose two evils, one in the eastern, the other in the western provinces. In the east the state dominated the church until it lost all energy and uplifting life. In the west, as we shall see, the church gradually usurped power over the state, and the result was not *Christianity* but a more or less corrupt *hierarchy* controlling the nations of Europe, making the church mainly a political machine.

CHAPTER X.

THE IMPERIAL CHURCH.

PART TWO.

THE FOUNDING OF CONSTANTINOPLE. THE DIVI-
SION OF THE EMPIRE. THE SUPPRESSION OF
HEATHENISM. THE CONTROVERSIES
AND COUNCILS. THE RISE OF
MONASTICISM.

Soon after Christianity was recognized as the religion of the Roman empire, a new capital was chosen, built, and established as the seat of authority—an event which brought to pass important results in the church, as well as in the state.

II. The Founding of Constantinople, 325 A. D.

Constantine recognized that Rome was closely associated with the heathen worship, filled with temples and statues, strongly inclined to the old religion, a city controlled by pagan traditions. Moreover, its situation in the midst of a great plain left it open to attack from enemies. In the earlier times of the republic the city had been more than once beseiged by foreign foes; and in its later history, armies from the provinces had many times enthroned and dethroned emperors. In the system of government organized by Diocletian and continued by Constantine, there was no place for even

1. Need of a New Capital

the shadowy authority of the Roman senate. The emperors now possessed unlimited power; and Constantine sought a capital untrammeled by traditions and especially under the auspices of the new religion.

2. Its Location.

Constantine showed great wisdom in the choice of his new capital. He selected the Greek City of Byzantium, which had been standing for a thousand years, situated at the meeting of Europe and Asia; where the continents are separated by two narrow straits, on the north the Bosphorus, and on the south the Hellespont (now Dardanelles), together sixty miles long, generally less than a mile wide and nowhere more than four miles wide. The site of the city is so fortified by nature, that in all its history of more than twenty-five centuries, it has rarely been taken by enemies, while its rival Rome has been overcome and ravaged many times. Here Constantine fixed his capital and planned the great city universally known for many years as Constantinople, "the city of Constantine," but now officially called Istanbul.

3. Capital and Church.

In the new capital the emperor and the patriarch (which was the title subsequently given to the chief bishop of Constantinople) dwelt side by side. The church was honored, but was overshadowed by the authority of the throne. Partly from the presence and power of the emperor, but also from the pliant, submissive nature of its people, the church in the eastern empire became mainly the servant of the state, although at times patriarchs like John Chrysostom asserted their independence.

In the new capital were no temples to idols, but soon many churches arose. Of these the largest was named Sancta Sophia. "Sacred Wisdom." It was built by Constantine, but after its destruction by fire, was rebuilt by the emperor Justinian (537 A. D.) on a magnificent scale, surpassing any other church of its day. It remained the leading cathedral of Christendom for eleven centuries, until 1453 A. D., when the city was taken by the Turks. Then in one day it became a mosque, as it remains at present.

4. Sancta Sophia.

The division of the empire soon followed the building of the new capital. The boundaries were so wide and the danger of invasion from barbarians around was so imminent, that one emperor could no longer protect his vast dominions. Diocletian had begun the division of authority in 305 A. D.; Constantine also appointed associate emperors; and in the year 375 A. D. Theodosius completed the separation. From the time of Theodosius the Roman world was divided into Eastern and Western, separated by the Adriatic Sea. The Eastern empire was known as Greek, the Western as Latin, from the prevailing language in each section. The division of the empire was a foreboding of the coming disruption of the church.

III. Division of Roman Empire.

One of the most remarkable facts in history is the rapid transformation of a vast empire from the heathen to the Christian religion. Outwardly, at the opening of the fourth century, the old gods were entrenched in the reverence of the Roman world. But before the fifth century began, the

IV. Suppression of Heathenism.

temples had been abandoned to ruin or turned into churches, sacrifices and libations had ceased, and in profession the Roman empire was Christian. Let us now notice how heathenism fell from its lofty state.

1. Constantine Tolerant. Constantine was tolerant, both in temperament and from political motives, although emphatic in his recognition of the Christian religion. He sanctioned no sacrifices to the images formerly worshiped, and put an end to the offerings to the statue of the emperor. But he favored the toleration of all forms of religion, and sought the gradual conversion of his subjects to Christianity, through evangelization and not by compulsion. He retained some of the heathen titles of the emperor, as that of *pontifex maximus,* "chief priest"—a title by the way held by all the popes since. He continued also the support of the vestal virgins at Rome.

2. His Successors Intolerant. But Constantine's successors on the throne were intolerant. The conversion of the heathen was moving forward rapidly enough, even too rapidly for the well-being of the church. Yet the early Christian emperors after Constantine sought to accelerate the movement by a series of oppressive laws. **(1) Endowments of Temples Confiscated.** All endowments held by the temples and heathen priests, whether given by the state or by worshipers, were seized, and, in most places, transferred to the churches. **(2) Heathen Rites Interdicted.** The heathen sacrifices and rites of worship were forbidden, and their observance was made a penal offense. Not long after Constantine's reign his son ordered to all worshipers of idols the penalty of death and confiscation of their property.

Heathenism for a generation before its final suppression had a few martyrs; but very few in contrast with the number of Christian sufferers through two hundred years. Already many of the temples had been consecrated as churches; and after some years it was ordered that those still remaining should be torn down, unless needed for Christian worship. **(3) Temples Demolished.**

The command was issued that no one should write or speak against the Christian religion, and all books of its opposers should be burned. One result **(4) Anti-Christian Books.** of this edict has been that practically all our knowledge of the anti-Christian or heretical sects is obtained from books written against them. The enforcement of these repressive laws varied greatly in different portions of the empire; but their effect was that heathenism entirely passed away in the course of three or four generations.

As the long conflict of Christianity with heathenism was ending in victory, a new strife arose, a civil **V. Controversies and Councils.** war in the field of thought, a series of controversies within the church over its doctrines. While the church was fighting for its life against persecution, it remained united, although rumblings of doctrinal dissension were heard. But when the church was not only safe but dominant, sharp debate concerning doctrine arose, shaking its very foundations. During this period three great controversies were carried on, besides many lesser ones, and to settle these vexed questions councils of the whole church were called. At these councils only bishops were voting members. All the lower clergy and laity were expected to submit to their decisions.

1. The Arian Controversy.

The first controversy arose over the Doctrine of the Trinity, especially the relation of the Father and the Son. Arius, a presbyter of Alexandria, about 318 A. D., set forth the doctrine that Christ though higher than the human nature was inferior to God, and was not eternal in existence, but had a beginning. Against these views, the great champion was Athanasius, also of Alexandria. He asserted the unity of the Son with the Father, the deity of Christ and his eternal existence. The controversy extended throughout the church, and after Constantine had vainly endeavored to end the strife, he called a council of the bishops, meeting at Nicæa in Bithynia 325 A. D. Athanasius, at that time only a deacon, was permitted to speak, though not to vote, and was able to bring the majority of the council to condemn the teachings of Arius, in the Nicene creed. But Arius was politically powerful; his opinions were held by many of the upper classes, and by the son and successor of Constantine. Five times Athanasius was driven into exile, and as many times recalled. When a friend said to him, "Athanasius, you have the whole world against you," he answered "Be it so—Athanasius against the world—*Athanasius contra mundum.*" His last seven years were passed in peace at Alexandria, where he died in 373 A. D. His views finally, but not till long after his death, became supreme throughout the church both east and west. They are definitely set forth in the Athanasian Creed, formerly but not now believed to have been written by Athanasius.

Next came the controversy over the Nature of Christ. Apollinaris, bishop of Laodicea (360 A. D.), asserted that the divine nature took the place of the human nature in Christ; that Jesus on earth was not man, but God alone in human form. The majority of bishops and theologians held that the personality of Jesus Christ was a union of God and man, deity and humanity in one nature. The Apollinarian heresy was condemned by the Council of Constantinople, 381 A. D., and was followed by the withdrawal of Apollinaris from the church.

2. The Apollinarian Controversy

The only extended controversy of this period arising in the western church was over questions relating to sin and salvation. It began with Pelagius, a monk who came from Britain to Rome about 410 A. D. His doctrine was that we do not inherit our sinful tendencies from Adam, but that each soul makes its own choice, whether of sin or of righteousness; that every human will is free and every soul is responsible for its decisions. Against this view appeared the greatest intellect after St. Paul in the history of Christianity, the mighty Augustine, who held that Adam represented the entire race, that in Adam's sin all mankind sinned, and all mankind are held guilty; that man cannot accept salvation by his own choice, but only by the will of God, who chooses whom he will save. The Pelagian view was condemned by the Council of Carthage 418 A. D., and the theology of Augustine became the standard of orthodoxy in the church. Not until modern times, under Arminius in Holland

3. The Pelagian Controversy.

(about 1600) and John Wesley in the eighteenth century was there any serious breaking away from the Augustinian system of doctrine.

VI. The Rise of Monasticism. While these great controversies were raging, another movement began, which in the Middle Ages grew to immense proportions. This was the rise of the monastic spirit. In the early church were no monks nor nuns. The Christians lived in families, and though keeping apart from idolatrous associations, were still members of society in general. But in the period now under consideration we note the beginnings and early progress of a movement toward the monastic life.

1. Its Origin. After Christianity became dominant in the empire, worldliness crept into the church and became prevalent. Many who sought a higher life were dissatisfied with their surroundings, and retired from the world. Either alone or in groups they dwelt in seclusion, seeking to cultivate the spiritual life by meditation, prayer, and ascetic habits. This monastic spirit began in Egypt, where it was fostered by the warm climate and the few necessities for living.

2. Its Founder. Instances of the solitary life may be found early in Christian history; but we may consider Anthony as its founder about 320 A. D., for his life first attracted general attention and led to thousands of followers. He lived for years alone in a cave in Egypt, was widely known, and held in reverence for the purity and simplicity of his character. Multitudes followed his example, and the caves of upper Egypt were thronged by his disciples. They were called "anchorites" from a word meaning "retirement." Those who formed themselves into communities were called "cenobites," From Egypt the spirit spread over the eastern church, where the monastic life was adopted by multitudes of both men and women.

One peculiar form of asceticism was adopted by the pillar-saints, of whom the first was a Syrian monk, Simon, called Stylites, "of the pillar." He left the monastery in 423 A. D. and built in succession several pillars, each higher than its predecessor, the last one sixty feet high and four feet broad. On these pillars in turn he lived for thirty-seven years. Thousands emulated his life, and Syria held many pillar-saints between the fifth and twelfth centuries. But this form of life never obtained followers in Europe.

3. Pillar-Saints.

The monastic movement in Europe spread more slowly than in Asia and Africa. The individual, solitary life of the ascetic soon gave place in Europe to the establishment of monasteries, where work was united with prayer. Benedict's Rule, by which the western monasteries were generally organized and directed, was promulgated in 529 A. D. The monastic spirit grew through the Middle Ages, and will be noticed again in the history.

4. Monasticism in Europe.

CHAPTER XI.

THE IMPERIAL CHURCH.

PART THREE.

GROWTH OF POWER IN THE ROMAN CHURCH.
DOWNFALL OF WESTERN ROMAN EMPIRE.
LEADERS OF THE PERIOD.

VII. Growing Power of Roman Church.

We have seen the city of Rome supplanted by Constantinople as the capital of the world. We shall now see Rome asserting its right to be the capital of the church. Throughout this period the Roman Church was gaining in prestige and power, and the Bishop of Rome, now entitled pope, was claiming the throne of authority over all the Christian world, and recognized as head of the church in all Europe west of the Adriatic Sea. This progress did not as yet reach the overweening demand of power over the *state* as well as over the church, which was manifested in the Middle Ages, but was strongly tending in that direction. Let us ascertain some of the causes promoting this movement.

Causes.

. Analogy of Imperial Rule.

The likeness of the church as an organization to the empire powerfully strengthened the tendency toward one head. In a state governed not from below by election, but from above as an autocracy, where one emperor ruled with absolute power, it was natural that the church should be governed in the same manner, having one head. Everywhere bishops controlled the churches, but the question was constantly arising—who should control the bishops? What bishop should take the place of an emperor over the church? The presiding bishops in certain cities soon came to be called "metropolitans," and afterward "patriarchs." There were patriarchs at Jerusalem, Antioch, Alexandria, Constantinople, and Rome. The Roman bishop took the title of "papa, father," afterward modified into *pope*. Between these five patriarchs were frequent contests for precedence and supremacy; but the question finally narrowed down to the choice between the patriarch of Constantinople and the pope of Rome, as head of the church.

Rome asserted apostolic authority for its claim. Rome was the only church which could name as its founder two apostles, and these the greatest of all the apostles, St. Peter and St. Paul. The tradition arose that Peter was the first bishop of Rome, whether true or false is uncertain. As bishop, Peter must have been pope. It was assumed that in the first century the title "Bishop" meant the same as in the fourth century, a ruler over the clergy and the church; and that Peter, as chief of the apostles, must have possessed authority over the whole church. Two texts in the gospels were quoted as warrant for this claim. One of these may now be seen written in gigantic letters in Latin, around the dome of St. Peter's Church in Rome "Thou art Peter; and on this Rock I will build my

2. Assertion of Apostolic Sanction.

Matt. 16:18.

church." The other is "Feed my sheep." It was argued that if Peter was the first head of the church, then his successors, the popes of Rome, must continue his authority.

3. Character of Roman Church and Bishop.

(1) The Bishops.

The character of the Roman Church and its early heads strongly supported these claims. The bishops at Rome were in the main, and in far greater measure than those in Constantinople, strong, wise, forceful men, who made themselves felt throughout the church. Much of the old imperial quality which had made Rome the mistress of the world still dwelt in the Roman nature. Herein Rome stood in contrast with Constantinople. Originally, Rome had made the emperors; while the emperors had made Constantinople, and peopled it with submissive subjects. The church at Rome had always been conservative in doctrine, little influenced by sects and heresies; standing as a pillar for the orthodox teaching. This trait greatly added to its influence in the church at large.

(2) The Church at Rome Orthodox.

(3) Practical Christianity of Roman Church.

Then, too, the church at Rome showed practical Christianity. No church excelled it in care for the poor, not only among its own members, but even for the needy among the heathen in times of famine or pestilence. It had given liberal aid to persecuted churches in other provinces. When a heathen official at Rome demanded the treasures of the church, the bishop assembled its poor members, saying, "These are our treasures."

4. The Transfer of the Capital.

The transfer of the capital from Rome to Constantinople, instead of lessening the influence of the Roman bishop or pope, greatly increased it. We have seen that in Constantinople the emperor and his court dominated the church; the patriarch was generally subservient to the imperial palace. But in Rome there was no emperor to outrank and over-awe the pope; he was the greatest potentate in that region. Europe had always looked to Rome with reverence; now that the capital was far away, and especially as the empire itself was in collapse, the feeling of loyalty toward the Roman pontiff began to take the place of that toward the Roman emperor.

Thus it came to pass that throughout the west, the Roman bishop or pope, as the head of the Roman Church, was regarded as the leading authority in the general church. For instance, at the Council of Chalcedon in Asia Minor (451 A. D.), Rome was placed first and Constantinople second. The way was being paved for the still higher assumptions of Rome and the pope in the ages to follow.

Throughout this period of the Imperial Church, however, another movement was in progress, that mightiest catastrophe in all history, the downfall of the western Roman Empire. In the reign of Constantine outwardly the realm seemed as well protected and impregnable as it had been in the reign of Marcus Aurelius or of Augustus. Yet it was honey-combed with moral and political decay, and ready to collapse under invaders from every side who were eager to prey upon it. Within twenty-five years after Constantine's death in 337 A. D. the barriers on the border of the western empire were broken down, and hordes of barba-

VIII. The Downfall of Western Roman Empire.

rians (a name applied by the Romans to all peoples except themselves, the Greeks and the Jews) were everywhere pouring in upon the helpless provinces, seizing territory and establishing independent kingdoms. In less than a hundred and forty years the western Roman Empire, which had endured a thousand years, and whose subject peoples were contented under its sway, was swept out of existence. It is not difficult to find the causes of this stupendous overthrow.

1. Causes of its Overthrow.
(1) Its Riches Coveted.

The riches of the empire were coveted by its barbarian neighbors. On one side of a boundary were wealthy cities living at ease, vast fields with harvests, peoples possessing all things desired by the poorer, uncivilized, wandering, but warlike, tribes just over the border. For centuries before the barbarian inroads, the main business of the Roman emperors had been the defense of the frontiers against the threatened attacks of these enemies. The sole reason for having several emperors reigning jointly, was the need, near these points of danger, of a ruler clothed with authority, who could act without waiting for orders from a distant capital.

(2) Romans Unused to War.

Even at their best the Romans were evenly matched by the barbarians, man for man; and through centuries of peace, they had grown unused to war. In our time the civilized nations possess munitions of war far superior to those of the savage tribes; but in ancient days, both sides fought with swords and spears, and the only advantage of the Romans lay in the superb discipline of their legions. But that discipline was greatly relaxed in the times of the later emperors; and the barbarians were physically the stronger, the bolder, and more apt in warfare. What was worse for the degnerate Romans, they no longer served in their own armies. The legions were manned by these very barbarians, who for a time often fought in defense of Rome against their own people. Most of the later armies, their generals, and even many of the emperors themselves came from the barbarian races. No people can long maintain their liberties who habitually hire foreigners to do their fighting when fighting is necessary.

The empire, not too strong in its resources of men, was also weakened by civil wars, carried on through generations by claimants to the imperial throne. The emperors were no longer chosen by the senate, but when one was slain (as most of them were) each army in a different province set up its own candidate, and the decision was not by votes but by arms. In ninety years eighty leaders were hailed as emperor and claiming the throne. At one time the emperors, so called, were so many as to be called "the thirty tyrants." Cities were plundered, armies were extravagantly paid, and the whole empire was impoverished by the ambition of men for power. As a result, garrisons were called away from the borders, and the land was left open and helpless against the barbarian invaders. (3) Empire Weakened by Civil Wars.

The immediate cause of many invasions lay in the movement of Asiatic tribes. When the barbarians on the east of the European provinces (4) Movement of Asiatic Tribes.

burst in upon the Romans, they declared that they had been driven from their own homes by the oncoming of an irresistible host of strange warriors accompanied by their families, who had changed their habitations from the interior of Asia. These people were called in general Huns. What led them to forsake their homes in central Asia cannot be fully known; but is believed to have been a change in the climate and a lack of rain, turning fertile areas into deserts. Later, these Huns, under their fierce king Attila, came into direct contact with the Romans, and proved the most terrible of all their foes.

2. The Invading Tribes.

As ours is a history not of the Roman Empire but of the Christian church, our account of these successive invading tribes must be a brief outline. The earlier invasions were from races between the Danube River and the Baltic Sea. The Visigoths (West Goths) led by their chieftain Alaric swept over Greece and Italy, captured and spoiled Rome, and set up a kingdom in southern France. The Vandals under Genseric marched across France to Spain, and thence into northern Africa, conquering these countries. The Burgundians crossed the Rhine, and established a kingdom having Strassburg as its center. The Franks, a German tribe, seized all northern Gaul, which they named Francia. A later king of the Franks, Clovis, became a Christian, and was followed by his people; and the Franks greatly aided in the conversion of northern Europe, largely by force, to the Christian religion. The Saxons and Angles from Denmark and the lands northward, finding that Britain had been deserted

(1) Visigoths (Alaric), 376.

(2) Vandals (Genseric), 406.

(3) Burgundians, 414.

(4) Franks, 420.

Clovis, 481.

(5) Saxons and Angles, 440.

PIAZZA AND CHURCH OF ST. PETER, ROME. TRADITIONAL BURIAL-PLACE OF THE APOSTLE PETER. VATICAN PALACE, RESIDENCE OF THE POPE, ON THE RIGHT

THE SEIZURE OF POPE BONIFACE VIII, 1303

by the Roman legions, made inroads, generation after generation, and almost extirpated the ancient Christianity, until the Anglo-Saxon kingdom itself was converted through missionaries from Rome.

About 450 A. D. the terrible Huns, under their merciless king, Attila, invaded Italy, and threatened to destroy not only the Roman empire, but with it the kingdoms set up within its borders.   Goths, Vandals and Franks, under the leadership of Rome, united against them; a great battle was fought at Chalons in northern France, the Huns were defeated with terrible slaughter, and by the death of Attila soon after, their power came to an end.   The battle at Chalons (451 A. D.) decided that Europe should not be overrun and ruled by Asiatics, but should develop into its own civilization. **(6) Huns (Attila), 450** **Battle of Chalons, 451.**

By these successive invasions and disruptions, the once vast empire of Rome was reduced to a little territory around the capital.   In 476 A. D. a comparatively small tribe of Germans, the Heruli, under their King Odoacer, took possession of the city, and dethroned the boy-emperor—whose name by a curious coincidence, combined those of the founder and of the first emperor, Romulus Augustus, nicknamed "Augustulus, Augustus the Little." Odoacer took the title "King of Italy," and from that year, 476 A. D., the western Roman Empire was no more.   From the foundation of the city and the state (said to have been in 753 B. C.) to the fall of the empire, was twelve hundred years.   The eastern empire, having Constantinople for its capital, endured until 1453 A. D. **3. The Fall of Rome, 476 A. D.**

4. The
Church
and the
Barbarians.

Nearly all these invading tribes in their home lands had been heathen. An exception was the Goths, who had been already converted to Arian Christianity, and had the Bible in their own language, of which the portions still extant form the earliest Teutonic literature. Nearly all these conquering tribes became Christians, partly through the Goths, but more through the people among whom they settled, and in time the Arians became orthodox believers. The Christianity of that decadent age was still vital and aggressive, and won these conquering races. In turn, their vigorous blood contributed to make a new European race. We have already seen that the decline and fall of the imperial power at Rome only increased the influence throughout Europe of the Roman Church and the popes. Thus, although the empire fell, the church still showed itself imperial.

IX. Leaders
of the Period.

We must now name some of the leaders in this period of the Imperial Church.

1. Athanasius,
293-373.

Athanasius (293-373 A. D.) was the great defender of the faith in the opening of the period. We have seen how he arose to prominence in the Arian controversy, and was the chief debater, though not a voter, in the Council of Nicæa, 325; soon after bishop of Alexandria, when thirty-three years old; five times exiled, but ever battling for the faith; and finally ending his life in peace and honor.

2. Ambrose,
340-397.

Ambrose of Milan (340-397 A. D.), the earliest of the Latin fathers, was elected bishop while a layman, not even baptized but receiving instruction for membership. Both Arians and orthodox united in his election. He became a commanding figure in the Church; rebuked the emperor, Theodosius, for a cruel act, and compelled him to make confession and do penance; afterward was treated with the highest regard by the emperor, and was chosen to preach his funeral sermon. He was the author of many books, but his greatest honor was in receiving into the church the mighty Augustine.

John, surnamed Chrysostom, "the golden mouth," because of his matchless eloquence, the greatest preacher of the period, was born at Antioch in 345 A. D.; became bishop or patriarch of Constantinople 398, and preached to vast congregations in the Church of St. Sophia. But his fidelity, independence, reforming zeal, and courage displeased the court. He was banished, and died in exile 407 A. D., but after his death was vindicated; and his body was brought back to Constantinople and buried in honor. He was a mighty preacher, a statesman, and an able expositor of the Bible.

3. John Chrysostom, 345-407.

Jerome (340–420 A. D.) was the most learned of the Latin fathers. He received at Rome an education in literature and oratory, but renounced worldly honors for a religious life, strongly tinged with asceticism. He established a monastery at Bethlehem, and lived there for many years. Of his numerous writings, the one of most far-reaching influence was his translation of the Bible into the Latin language, a work known as the Vulgate, i. e., the Bible in common speech, which is still the authorized Bible of the Roman Catholic Church.

4. Jerome, 340-420.

5. Augustine 354-430. The most eminent name in all this period is that of Augustine, who was born 354 A. D. in northern Africa. In young manhood he was a brilliant scholar, but worldly, ambitious and pleasure-loving. At the age of thirty-three he became a Christian through the influence of his mother Monica, the teaching of Ambrose of Milan, and the study of St. Paul's epistles. He was made bishop of Hippo in northern Africa in 395, just as the barbarian invasions were beginning. Among his many works his "City of God" was a magnificent plea for Christianity to take the place of the dissolving empire; and his "Confessions" are a deep revelation of his own heart and life. But his fame and his influence rest upon his writings on Christian theology, of which Augustine was the greatest expositor since St. Paul. He died in 430 A. D.

OUTLINE OF CHAPTERS XII, XIII, XIV, XV, XVI, XVII.

FOURTH GENERAL PERIOD. THE MEDIEVAL CHURCH.

From the Fall of Rome, 476 A. D.,
To the Fall of Constantinople, 1453 A. D.

I. PROGRESS OF THE PAPAL POWER (CHAPTER XII).

1. The Stage of Growth, 590-1073.

Causes:

    (1) A Power for Righteousness.
    (2) Uncertainties of Secular Rule.
    (3) Constancy of Church Rule.
    (4) Medieval "Pious Frauds."
        (a) Forged Donation of Constantine.
        (b) False Decretals of Isidore.
        (c) Evidences of Forgery.

2. The Stage of Culmination, 1073-1216.

    (1) Rule of Hildebrand (Gregory VII).
        (a) The Clergy Reformed.
        (b) The Church Freed from State.
        (c) The Church Supreme.

    (2) Rule of Innocent III, 1198-1216.
        (a) His Claims.
        (b) Choice of Emperor.
        (c) Rule in Rome.
        (d) Submission of French King.
        (e) Submission of English King.

3. The Stage of Decline.

    (1) Boniface VIII, 1303.
    (2) Babylonish Captivity, 1305-1378.
    (3) Council of Constance, 1414.

II. RISE OF MOHAMMEDAN POWER (CHAPTER XIII).

1. Its Founder, Mohammed, 570-632.
2. His Religion.
3. Progress of Islam.
4. Its Elements of Power.

    (1) Arab Faith.
    (2) Submissiveness of Asiatic Greeks.
    (3) Character of Islamite Religion.

5. Favorable Aspects of Mohammedanism.
   (1) Simplicity of Doctrine.
   (2) Opposition to Image Worship.
   (3) Rejection of Priestly and Saintly Mediation.
   (4) Abstinence from Strong Drink.
   (5) Early Promotion of Literature and Science.

6. Unfavorable Aspects of Mohammedanism.
   (1) Conversion by Conquest.
   (2) Religion Secularized.
   (3) View of God.
   (4) View of Christ.
   (5) Conception of Heaven.
   (6) Degradation of Womanhood.
   (7) Lack of Statesmanship.

III. THE HOLY ROMAN EMPIRE (CHAPTER XIV).

1. Its Founder. Charlemagne, 742-814.
2. The Empire.
3. Great Emperors.
4. The Emperors and the Popes.
5. Decline and Fall of the Empire.

IV. SEPARATION OF LATIN AND GREEK CHURCHES (CHAPTER XIV).

1. Doctrinal Cause.
2. Causes in Rule and Usage.
3. Political Cause.
4. Claims of Rome.

V. THE CRUSADES, 1095-1270 (CHAPTER XV).

1. Their Origin.
2. The Seven Crusades.
   (1) First Crusade, 1095-1099. Godfrey of Bouillon.
   (2) Second Crusade, 1147-1149. Louis VII, Conrad III.
   (3) Third Crusade, 1189-1191. Frederick, Philip, Richard.
   (4) Fourth Crusade, 1201-1204 (Constantinople).
   (5) Fifth Crusade, 1228, 1229. Frederick II.
   (6) Sixth Crusade, 1248-1254. Louis IX.
   (7) Seventh Crusade, 1270-1272. Louis IX.

3. Causes of Failure.
   (1) Quarrels of Leaders.
   (2) Limited Views.

6. Good Results of the Crusades.

    (I) Pilgrims Protected.
    (2) Moslem Aggressions Checked.
    (3) Acquaintance among Nations.
    (4) Impulse to Trade.
    (5) Effects on Power of the Church.

VI. DEVELOPMENT OF MONASTICISM (CHAPTER XVI).

1. The Monastic Orders.

    (1) Benedictines, 529.   St. Benedict.
    (2) Cistercians, 1098.   St. Robert, St. Bernard.
    (3) Franciscans, 1209.   St. Francis.
    (4) Dominicans, 1215.   St. Dominic.

2. Some Benefits of Monasticism.

    (1) Centers of Peace.
    (2) Hospitality.
    (3) Refuge to Helpless.
    (4) Agriculture.
    (5) Literature.
    (6) Education.
    (7) Missions.

3. Some Evil Results of Monasticism (Chapter XV).

    (1) Exaltation of Celibacy.
    (2) Effects on Social and National Life.
    (3) Luxury and Immorality.
    (4) Contributions Extolled.

VII. MEDIEVAL ART AND LITERATURE (CHAPTER XVI).

1. Universities.
2. Cathedrals.
3. Awakening of Literature.
4. Awakening of Art.

VIII. BEGINNING OF RELIGIOUS REFORM (CHAPTER XVII).

1. Albigenses, 1170.
2. Waldensians, 1170.
3. John Wyclif, 1324-1384.
4. John Huss, 1369-1415.
5. Jerome Savonarola, 1452-1498.

IX. THE FALL OF CONSTANTINOPLE, 1453 (CHAPTER XVII).

X. SCHOLARS AND LEADERS (CHAPTER XVII).

1. Anselm, 1033-1109.
2. Abelard, 1079-1142.
3. Bernard of Clairvaux, 1091-1163.
4. Thomas Aquinas, 1226-1274.

WORKS FOR FURTHER STUDY.

Cowan. Landmarks of Church History, Chaps. IX-XXIV.
Selden. Story of the Christian Centuries, pp. 95-152.
Zenos. Compendium of Church History, pp. 107-197.
Sohm. Outlines of Church History, pp. 74-145.
Moncrief. Short History of the Christian Church, pp. 161-278.
Epochs of Church History:

    The Age of Charlemagne. C. L. Wells.
    The Age of Hildebrand. M. R. Vincent.
    The Age of the Crusades. J. M. Ludlow.
    The Age of the Renascence. Paul Van Dyke.
    The Age of the Great Western Schism. Clinton Locke.

Fisher. History of the Christian Church, pp. 144-286.
Hurst. History of the Christian Church, Vol. I, pp. 465-949.
Schaff. History of the Christian Church, Vols. IV, V.
George Eliot (Marian Evans). Romola. (Fiction.)

CHAPTER XII.

THE MEDIEVAL CHURCH.

PART ONE.

FROM THE FALL OF ROME, 476 A. D., TO THE FALL
OF CONSTANTINOPLE, 1453 A. D.   PROGRESS
OF THE PAPAL POWER.

In this period of nearly a thousand years, our
interest will be directed upon the Western or Latin
Church, having the seat of its authority in Rome,
still the imperial city, although its political power
had passed away.   Little attention will be given to
the Greek Church, ruled from Constantinople,
except as its affairs relate to the history of European
Christianity.   We do not recite events in their
chronological order, but survey great movements,
often parallel with each other.

The development of papal power is the great I. Progress
outstanding fact in the ten centuries of the Middle of the Papal Power.
Ages.   We have already seen how the Pope of
Rome claimed to be "Universal Bishop," and head of
the church; we shall now see him claiming to be
ruler over the *nations*, above kings and emperors.
This development had three stages—Growth, Culmination, and Decline.

The stage of growth in the papal power began 1. The Stage
with the pontificate of Gregory I, "the Great," and of Growth, 590-1073.

came to its height under Gregory VII, better known as Hildebrand. It is to be noted that from early times each pope on assuming his office changed his name; and Gregory VII is the only pope whose family name stands out in history after his elevation. Gregory I was the ecclesiastic of whom the well-known story is told, that seeing some fair-haired, blue-eyed captives in Rome, and asking who they were, was answered "Angli" (English); he said "Non Angli, sed angeli; not Angles, but angels." Afterward, when he became pope, he sent missionaries to England for the Christianization of its people. He extended the realm of the church by an active interest in the conversion of the nations in Europe, still remaining heathen, and in bringing over to the orthodox faith the Arian Visigoths in Spain. Gregory withstood successfully the claim of the Patriarch of Constantinople to the title of Universal Bishop. He made the church virtual ruler in the province around Rome, thus paving the way for temporal power. He also developed certain doctrines of the Roman Church, especially the adoration of images, purgatory and transubstantiation, or the belief that in the mass or communion the bread and wine are miraculously transformed into the veritable body and blood of Christ. He was a strong advocate of the monastic life, having himself been a monk. Gregory I was one of the ablest administrators in the history of the Roman church, and well deserved his title of "the Great." Under a series of popes through hundreds of years the authority of the Roman pontificate was advanced

Gregory I, " The Great," 590-604.

and generally recognized.   Certain causes may be
named for this growing power of the popedom.

One reason why the rule of the Roman See Causes of
was so widely accepted was that in the earlier ages Papal Power.
of this period, the influence of the popes was mainly
a power for righteousness.   The church stood (1) A Power
between princes and their subjects, to curb tyranny for Right-
and injustice, to protect the weak, and to demand eousness.
the rights of the people.   In the palaces more than
one ruler was compelled to take back an unjustly
discarded wife, and to observe at least the outward
forms of decency.   There were many exceptions,
popes who flattered wicked princes, but the general
spirit of the papacy in the earlier Middle Ages, was
in favor of good government.

The rivalries and uncertainties of secular rule (2) Uncer-
were in marked contrast with the steadiness and tainties of
uniformity of the churchly government.   During Secular Rule.
most of these ages Europe was in a solvent condition, with rulers rising and falling, castle at war
with castle, and no extensive enduring authority.
The old empire fell in the fifth century and Europe
was almost in chaos until the ninth century, when
the empire of Charlemagne was established.   Most
of his immediate successors were weak men, many of
them sought the aid of Rome, and were ready to
give concessions of power to obtain it.   When once
power had been gained by the church at the expense
of the state, it was firmly held.

While the rule of states was changing, against it (3) Constancy
was the constant empire of the church.   During all of Church
those centuries of flux, and varying conditions, the Rule.

church stood firm, the one settled, steady institution. The claims of Rome to domination were almost invariably supported by the clergy, from the archbishop down to the humblest priest. During the Middle Ages, as we shall see later, there was an enormous growth of monasticism, and the monks and their abbots sided with priests and bishops in every contest for power. The church had its strong allies everywhere, and they never failed to advance its interests.

(4) Medieval "Pious Frauds."

Strange as the fact may seem to us, in the Middle Ages a number of "pious frauds" were put forth to support the authority of Rome. In an intelligent, scientific time, these would have been investigated, disproved, and discredited. But the scholarship of the medieval centuries was not critical; no one questioned the truth of the documents; they were widely circulated, everywhere accepted, and through them the claims of Rome were strongly buttressed. Centuries passed away before even the suggestion was made, that these foundations rested upon falsehood and not upon truth.

(a) The Forged Donation of Constantine.

One of these forged documents was the "Donation of Constantine." Long after the fall of the Roman Empire in Europe a document was circulated purporting to show that Constantine, the first Christian emperor, had given to the bishop of Rome, Sylvester I (314–335 A. D.), supreme authority over all the European provinces of the empire, and proclaimed the bishop of Rome as ruler even above the emperors. The document gave as the reason for removing the capital from Rome to Constantinople, that the emperor would allow no potentate to remain in Rome as a rival to the pope.

Of far greater influence was another forgery or series of forgeries, the False Decretals of Isidore, published about 830 A. D. These professed to be decisions given out by early bishops of Rome, from the apostles downward, setting forth the highest claims, such as the absolute supremacy of the pope of Rome over the universal church; the independence of the church from the state; the inviolability of the clergy of every rank from any accountability to the state; to the extent that no secular court could judge in matters pertaining to the clergy or the church. (b) False Decretals of Isidore.

In uncritical ignorant ages these documents were accepted without question, and for hundreds of years formed a bulwark to Roman claims. No one doubted the authenticity of these writings until the twelfth century, when the church was already anchored in power; and only with the dawn of the Reformation in the sixteenth century were their claims examined and shown to be unfounded. Some of the evidences against them were the following:

Their language was not the early Latin of the first and second centuries, but the corrupt and mixed tongue of the eighth and ninth centuries. The titles and historical conditions referred to were not those of the empire, but those of the Middle Ages, far different. The frequent quotations from Scripture were from the Vulgate (Latin) Bible, which was not translated until 400 A. D. A letter was given in full purporting to have been written (c) Evidences of Forgery.

by Victor, bishop of Rome 200 A. D., to Theophilus, bishop of Alexandria, who lived 400 A. D. What would be thought in our time as to the genuineness of a letter purporting to be from Queen Elizabeth to George Washington?

The growth of papal power while upward was not constant. There were strong princes who resisted it, as well as weak princes who submitted to it. Some of the popes were weak, and others were wicked, especially between 850 and 1050 A. D.; and these brought their office into discredit, even very near the time of its highest pitch of supremacy.

2. Stage of Culmination in Papal Power, 1073-1216.

The stage of culmination was between 1073 and 1216 A. D., about one hundred and fifty years, when the papacy stood in well-nigh absolute power, not only over the church but over the nations of Europe.

(1) Hildebrand, Pope Gregory VII.

This height was attained during the rule of Hildebrand, the only pope better known by his family name than by that assumed as pope, Gregory VII. Hildebrand really ruled the church as the power behind the throne for more than twenty years before he wore the triple crown, and afterward during his popedom, until his death in 1085. Some of his achievements may be named.

(a) Clergy Reformed.

Hildebrand reformed the clergy, which had become demoralized; broke up—but only for a time—simony, or the purchase of offices in the church; lifted the standard of morals throughout the clergy; and compelled the celibacy of the priesthood, which had been urged but until his day not enforced.

He freed the church from the domination of the (b) Church Freed.
state, by putting an end to the nomination of
popes and bishops by kings and emperors; and by
requiring all accusations against priests or involving
the church to be tried in ecclesiastical courts. It
had been the custom for the bishop at his consecration to receive a staff and ring from his sovereign, and to pledge feudal allegiance to him as his
lord secular. This practically made the bishops
appointees of the ruler. Hildebrand forbade the
presentation and the pledge.

He made the church supreme over the state. (c) Church Supreme.
The emperor, Henry IV, having taken offense at
Pope Gregory, summoned a synod of German
bishops, and induced (or compelled) them to vote
the deposition of the pope. Gregory retaliated
with an excommunication, absolving all the subjects
of Henry IV from their allegiance. Henry found
himself absolutely powerless under the papal ban.
In January, 1077, the emperor "having laid aside
all belongings of royalty, with bare feet and clad in
wool, continued for three days to stand before the
gate of the castle,"* at Canossa in northern Italy,
where the pope was staying, in order to make his
submission and receive absolution. It must be
added, however, that no sooner did Henry regain
power, than he made war on the pope, and drove
him out of Rome. Hildebrand died soon after,
leaving this testimony, "I have loved righteousness
and hated iniquity, and therefore I die in exile."

---

* These are the words of Pope Gregory VII, himself, in reporting the event.
Hence the expression "to go to Canossa," meaning submission to the pope or the
church.

But the record of the pope's triumph was more influential than that of his later defeat.

Gregory VII did not aim to abolish the rule of the state, but to subordinate it to the rule of the church, and of the pope as the church's head. He desired the secular power to govern the people, but under the higher jurisdiction of the spiritual kingdom, as he regarded it.

(2) Innocent III, 1198-1216.

(a) His Claims.

Another pope whose reign showed the high-water mark of power, was Innocent III (1198–1216). He declared in his inaugural discourse, "The successor of St. Peter stands midway between God and man; below God, above man; Judge of all, judged of none." In one of his official letters he wrote that to the pope "has been committed not only the whole church but the whole world," with "the right of finally disposing the imperial and all other crowns." Chosen to his office at the age of thirty-seven years, throughout his reign he maintained successfully these high assumptions.

(b) Choice of Emperor.

He chose for emperor Otho of Brunswick, who acknowledged publicly that he wore the crown "by the grace of God and the apostolic see." On account of Otho's insubordination he afterward deposed him, and caused another emperor to be chosen in his place. He assumed the government of the city of Rome, making rules for its officers, with himself as their supreme lord; thus in effect establishing a state under direct papal government, the forerunner of the "States of the Church." He compelled the licentious Philip Augustus, king of France, to receive back his wife, whom he had unrighteously

(c) Rule in Rome.

(d) Submission of French King.

divorced.   He excommunicated King John of Eng- (e) Submission of English King. land, compelled him to surrender his crown to the papal legate, and to receive it again as the pope's subject.   Innocent III may be regarded as greatest of all the popes in autocratic power; but he would not have possessed his authority if Hildebrand had not been great before him.

But as Europe was emerging from the twilight 3. Stage of Decline in Papal Power. of the Middle Ages, and national loyalty arose to compete with ecclesiastical, the decline of papal power began with Boniface VIII in 1303.   He made (1) Boniface VIII, 1303. claims as lofty as any of his predecessors, but found them ignored.   Boniface forbade Edward I of England to tax church property and priestly revenues, but was compelled to yield to the king, though with a form of compromise, by which the priests and bishops *gave* a part of their incomes for the needs of the kingdom.   He quarreled with Philip the Fair of France, who made war, seized the pope, and thrust him in prison.   Though released, he soon after died of grief.   From 1305, for more than seventy years, all the popes were chosen under the orders of the kings of France, and were subservient to their will.

The period from 1305 to 1378 is known as the (2) Babylonish Captivity, 1305-1378. Babylonish Captivity.   At the behest of the French king the seat of the papacy was transferred from Rome to Avignon, in the south of France.   The popes became figure-heads under French rule. Other aspirants to the popedom arose in Rome and elsewhere, popes and anti-popes in different lands.   Papal orders were disobeyed freely; excommunications were ignored; for example Edward III of England ordered the papal legate out of his kingdom.

(3) Council of Constance. In 1378 the reigning pope, Gregory XI, returned to Rome and in 1414 the Council of Constance was held to decide between the claims of four popes. All were deposed, and a new one was chosen. The popes from 1378 have continued dwelling at Rome, making claims as high as ever, but unable to enforce them.

CHAPTER XIII.

THE MEDIEVAL CHURCH.

PART TWO.

THE RISE OF MOHAMMEDAN POWER.

The movement which next claims our attention is the religion and empire founded by Mohammed in the opening of the seventh century; which tore away province after province from the Greek emperors of Constantinople unto its final extinction; brought the Eastern Church down to a subjection almost slavish; and even threatened the conquest of Europe. After thirteen centuries the Mohammedan faith still holds dominion over two hundred millions of people, and in one continent, that of Africa, is still growing. II. Rise of Mohamme-dan Power.

Its founder was Mohammed, born at Mecca, in Arabia, 570 A. D. He began his career as prophet and reformer in 610, when forty years old. At first disciples were won slowly, but his cause grew sufficiently to meet with persecution. He fled from Mecca in 622 A. D., and his flight, the Hegira, supplies the date from which the Mohammedan calendar is reckoned. He succeeded in bringing under his religion and authority the scattered Arabian tribes and returned as a conqueror to 1. Its Founder, Mohammed, 570-632.

Mecca. When he died, in 632 A. D., he was the accepted prophet and ruler throughout Arabia.

2. His Religion.

His religion is named Islam, "submission," that is, obedience to the will of God; and his followers are called Moslem, the name "Mohammedan" being never used by them. The articles of their faith, as stated by themselves are: that there is one God, whom they name Allah, the word being of common origin with the similar Hebrew word "Elohim;" that all events whether good or evil have been foreordained by God, consequently in every act they are carrying out God's will; that there are multitudes of angels, good and bad, invisible yet constantly dealing with men; that God has given his revelation in the Koran, a series of messages communicated to Mohammed through the Angel Gabriel, though they were not collected until after the prophet's death; that God has sent inspired prophets to men, of whom the four greatest have been Adam, Moses, Jesus, and, above all others, Mohammed; all the biblical prophets, the Christian apostles, and the saints who lived before Mohammed having been recognized and adopted as their own; that in the hereafter there will be a final resurrection, judgment, and heaven or hell for every man.

Doctrines.

(1) Unity of God.

(2) Fore-ordination.

(3) Angels.

(4) The Koran.

(5) Prophets.

(6) The Hereafter.

3. Progress of Islam

At first Mohammed relied on moral influences in preaching his gospel; but soon changed his methods and became a warrior, leading his united and fierce Arabs to the conquest of unbelievers. To each land or tribe they gave the alternatives of Islam, tribute, or death to those who resisted their arms.

Mohammed was succeeded by a series of caliphs who built up a vast empire by the sword. Palestine and Syria were soon conquered; and the holy places of Christianity fell under the power of Islam. (1) Palestine and Syria. Province after province of the Greco-Roman Empire was seized, and soon all that was left was the city of Constantinople, so that all the lands of the earliest Christianity became subject. (2) Asia Minor. Where the Christians submitted their worship was permitted under restrictions. Eastward the empire of the caliphs extended beyond Persia into India. (3) East of Persia. Their capital was at Bagdad on the Tigris. Westward, their conquests included Egypt, all northern Africa, and the greater part of Spain. (4) Egypt and North Africa. Nearly all this vast empire was gained within a hundred years after Mohammed's death. But its progress in western (5) Spain. Europe was stopped in southern France by Charles Martel, who rallied the discordant tribes under the leadership of the Franks, and won a decisive victory (6) Checked at Tours, 732. at Tours in 732 A. D. But for the battle of Tours, it is possible that all Europe might have been a Mohammedan continent, and the crescent have taken the place of the cross.

It is an interesting question—why did the Mohammedan religion and arms triumph over the oriental 4. Islam Elements of Power. world? We may name some of the causes. The earliest believers in Mohammed were the fierce, (1) Arab Faith and Courage. warlike Arabs, never conquered by a foreign foe, and following their prophet with a sincere, intense, all-conquering faith. They believed that they were accomplishing the will of God, and were destined to succeed. Everyone who fell in battle with the

unbelievers was destined to enter an immediate
heaven of sensual delight.   Against this virile,
unconquered, and conquering spirit was the weakened, submissive nature of the Asiatic Greeks.
From remote ages those lands had submitted
meekly to conquerors.   Their people had lost their
vigor, would rather surrender than draw the sword,
and pay tribute in preference to defending their
liberty.   Vast numbers of the population in the
Greek Empire were churchmen and monks, ready
to pray but not to fight.

(2) Greek Submissiveness.

The Islamite religion was far superior to the
paganism which it displaced in Arabia and the
lands east of that peninsula; and, it must be
admitted, stronger than the type of Christianity
which it met and overcame.   The Eastern Church,
unlike the Western, had long ceased missionary effort,
had lost its energy, and was inclined to speculation,
rather than to moral or spiritual effort.

(3) Islamite Religion.

In the religion of Mohammed at its best there
were, and still are to be found, some favorable
aspects, elements of value to the world.   One was
its simplicity of doctrine.   It believed in One God,
whom it was every man's duty to obey implicitly.
It had no mysterious intricate system of theology,
giving rise to interminable, useless controversies.
There was no need of scholarship to understand the
articles of the Mohammedan faith.   Another trait
of the Islamite religion was its opposition to image
worship.   Throughout the Christian world the
statues of the old gods and goddesses of Greece had
simply given place to images and pictures of the

5. Favorable Aspects.

(1) Simplicity of Doctrine.

(2) Opposition to Images.

Virgin Mary and the saints, worshiped in all the churches. The Moslems cast them out, destroyed them, and denounced all adoration of images whether carved or painted as idolatry. The Mohammedans rejected also all priestly and saintly mediation. The church of that world made salvation depend, not on simple faith in Christ and obedience to him as Lord, but on priestly rites and the intercession of departed saints. The Mohammedans swept all these away, and in their doctrine, brought every soul face to face with God. *(3) Rejection of Priestly and Saintly Mediation.*

Throughout the Moslem world is the rule of abstinence from strong drink. The first "temperance society" in the world's history was the Nazirites in Israel; and its successor on a larger scale was the Mohammedan religion, which forbade the faithful to drink wine or strong liquor. This is still held as a principle, but is not universally followed where Mohammedans live in contact with Europeans. *(4) Abstinence from Liquor.*

In the early period, under the caliphs, literature and science were promoted. The Arabians gave us the numerals, 1, 2, 3, etc., which were a great advance on the Roman system of notation through letters. In astronomy, they made one of the earliest catalogues of the stars. The court of the caliphs at Bagdad was a literary center. Mohammedan Spain was higher in culture and civilization than the Christian kingdoms of the period in that peninsula. But all intellectual progress ceased when the barbaric Turks succeeded the enlightened Saracens as leaders of the Mohammedan world. *6. Literature and Science.*

7. Unfavorable Aspects. Not to make our picture of Islam more favorable than the truth would warrant, we must notice on the other side wherein Mohammedanism has failed, its errors and its evils. Its primal wrong to humanity was in its method of missionary enterprise through the sword, promoting among men hate instead of love. Wherever a city resisted their conquest, its men were put to death, the women were placed in the harems of the victors, and the children were brought up in the Moslem faith. For many centuries the Turks made a regular practice of seizing untold thousands of Christian children, tearing them away from their parents, and bringing them up in distant provinces as bigoted Mussulmans.

(1) Conversion by Conquest.

(2) Religion Secularized. In the old Islamic conception the state and the church were absolutely one, and the government was expected to use its power to the utmost for the promotion of the true religion and the suppression of the false faith. Prior to World War I the Sultan of Turkey was also Caliph ("successor of Mohammed"). When Turkey became a republic the Sultan was dethroned and the Caliphate abolished. Other changes have taken place with the modernization of Turkey: One significant fact was the translation of the Koran into the vernacular. At Istanbul, in 1932, the Koran was read in the mosque of Sancta Sophia for the first time in Turkish.

(3) View of God. The Mohammedan conception of God is based on the Old rather than the New Testament. He is a fierce, relentless Oriental despot, with no love for humanity outside the followers of the Prophet.

Islam practically leaves Christ out of its doctrinal scheme. In the Mohammedan view he is not the Lord of the heavenly kingdom, the Son of God, the Saviour of men; but is reduced to the rank of a Jewish prophet, inferior in every respect to Mohammed. (4) View of Christ.

Its conception of heaven, the abode of the blessed in the life to come, is totally devoid of spirituality and altogether sensual. (5) Conception of Heaven.

One of the most debasing traits of the Mohammedan religion was its degradation of womanhood. Women were looked upon merely as the slaves or playthings of men. Modern Turkey has remedied this condition and in 1930 gave women the right to be electors and to be elected at municipal elections. But outside Turkey, women are held in small respect in the Mohammedan world. (6) Degradation of Womanhood.

In the field of history and politics, perhaps the most striking failure of the Mohammedan state has been in the realm of national administration. The Mohammedans were marvelous, almost miraculous, in their conquests, sweeping in a resistless torrent across continents from China to Spain. But they showed no power for wise, just government of the empires which they founded. Islamite lands were the worst governed on earth. Contrast the history of the Turks in this respect with that of the ancient Romans, who showed that they could not only win a great empire, but could rule it wisely, bringing prosperity to every land which they had conquered. (7) Lack of Statesmanship.

CHAPTER XIV.

THE MEDIEVAL CHURCH.

PART THREE.

THE HOLY ROMAN EMPIRE. THE SEPARATION OF LATIN AND GREEK CHURCHES.

III. The Holy Roman Empire, 800-1806 A. D.

From the ninth century until the ninteenth there existed in Europe a peculiar political organism, showing different phases during different generations, of which the official name was the Holy Roman Empire, commonly but inaccurately called the German Empire. Until it appeared, Europe west of the Adriatic Sea was in disorder ruled by warring tribes rather than by states. Yet, through all the confusion, the old Roman conception of unity and order remained, an aspiration after one empire to take the place of that which, though fallen, was still held in traditional veneration.

1. Its Founder, Charlemagne, 742-814.

In the latter part of the eighth century arose one of the greatest men of all time, Charles the Great (742-814 A. D.), claimed by the Germans as Karl the Great, and by the French as Charlemagne. He was the grandson of Charles Martel, the victor at Tours (732 A. D.); and King of the Franks, who were a Germanic tribe controlling a large part of France. Charles or Karl made himself the master of nearly all the lands in western Europe, northern

(122)

Spain, France, Germany, the Netherlands, Austria, and Italy, an empire indeed. While visiting Rome, on Christmas day in the year 800, he was crowned by Pope Leo III as Charles Augustus, Roman emperor, and was regarded as the successor of Augustus, Constantine, and the old Roman emperors. He reigned over all his wide dominion with power and wisdom, a conqueror, reformer, legislator, patron of education and of the church.

Crowned as Emperor, 800 A. D.

In theory his empire lasted a thousand years, but only for a short time was its authority over Europe real. The weakness and incapacity of Charlemagne's descendants, the varied development of different states, of languages, and conflicting national interests, caused the authority of the Holy Roman or German empire to be limited on the west mainly by the River Rhine. Even in Germany the minor states became practically independent, waged war with one another, and much of the time were only nominally under the emperor's control. The emperor was recognized as the titular head of European Christendom, and in France, England, and the Scandinavian states, he was honored, but not obeyed. Because his authority, such as it was, was limited to Germany, with a shadowy claim to Italy, his realm has been commonly called "the German Empire."

2. The Empire.

After the throne was lost by the degenerate descendants of Charlemagne, it became elective, the emperor being chosen by seven princes, entitled electors. Among the fifty-four emperors, we can merely name a few of the greatest after the time of

3. Great Emperors.

(1) Henry the Fowler, 919-936.

(2) Otho the Great, 951-973.

(3) Frederick Barbarossa, 1152-1190.

(4) Frederick II, 1196-1250.

(5) Rudolph of Hapsburgh, 1273-1291.

(6) Charles V, 1519-1556.

4. The Emperors and the Popes.

Charlemagne. Henry I (the Fowler), 919-936, began the restoration of the empire, which had fallen into decay, but his son Otho I (the Great), though not crowned as emperor until 951, and reigning until 973, is regarded as the real founder of the German Empire as distinct from the Roman. Frederick Barbarossa ("Red Beard") was one of the most powerful in the line of emperors. He went on the Third Crusade; but was drowned in Asia Minor, and his death led to the failure of the expedition. Frederick II, grandson of Barbarossa, has been called "the marvel and enigma of history, enlightened and progressive, the most liberal man of his age," in his views of government and religion; was twice excommunicated by the pope, but in the Fifth Crusade made himself king of Jerusalem. Rudolph of Hapsburgh, founder of the house of Austria, received the imperial crown in 1273, when it brought not much more than an empty title; but he compelled princes and barons to submit to his authority. From his time Austria was the most powerful state in the German confederation, and nearly all the emperors were his descendants, the archdukes of that country. Charles V, emperor at the opening of the Reformation (1519–1556) was also hereditary ruler of Austria, Spain, and the Netherlands. He did his best, but unavailingly, to hold all the lands under him to the old religion. In 1556 he voluntarily abdicated, and spent the last two years of his life in retirement.

For many centuries during the earlier history of the empire, there was strong rivalry, and sometimes open war between the emperors and the popes; emperors striving to rule the church, popes striving to rule the empire. We have seen how Pope Gregory VII (Hildebrand) for a time compelled the submission of an emperor, and how Innocent III set up and put down emperors and kings; but the strife grew less vigorous, and ceased after the Reformation, when the boundary lines between church and state had gradually become fixed.

As the realm of Austria grew more important, the emperors were increasingly occupied in their hereditary dominions. The many states 'of the empire became practically independent, until the emperorship was little more than a meaningless honor. In the eighteenth century, the cynical Voltaire said that "the Holy Roman empire was neither holy, nor Roman, nor an empire." The succession of emperors ended in 1806, when Napoleon was at the summit of his power. In that year Francis II was compelled to renounce the title "Emperor of the Holy Roman Empire," and assumed that of "Emperor of Austria." 5. Decline and Fall of the Empire.

The separation of the Latin and Greek churches was formally made in the eleventh century, although practically accomplished long before. Between popes and patriarchs strife had been the normal relation for hundreds of years, until finally, in 1054 A. D., the pope's messenger laid upon the altar of St. Sophia in Constantinople, the decree of excommunication; whereupon the patriarch in turn issued his decree excommunicating Rome and the churches submitting to the pope. Since that time IV. Separation of Latin and Greek Churches, 1054 A. D.

the Latin and Greek churches have stood apart, neither one recognizing the churchly existence of the other. Most of the questions at issue, forming causes leading to the separation, seem in our day almost trivial, yet for centuries these were subjects of violent controversy, and at times of bitter persecution.

1. Doctrinal Cause.

Doctrinally, the principal difference lay in the doctrine known as "the procession of the Holy Ghost." The Latins repeated it "the Holy Ghost proceeding from the Father *and the Son*"—in Latin "filioque." The Greeks said "from the Father" leaving out the word *filioque*. Over that one word mighty debates were held, books in untold numbers were written, and even blood was shed in bitter strife.

2. Causes in Rule and Usage.
(1) Priestly Marriage.

In the ceremonies of the church, different usages became the custom in the East and the West, and these customs were formulated into laws. The marriage of priests was forbidden in the western church, but sanctioned in the eastern. Throughout the Greek church at the present time, every village priest (who bears the title of "pope," equivalent to "father" among the Roman Catholics) must be a married man.

(2) Adoration of Images.

In the western churches the adoration of images has been practiced for a thousand years, while in the Greek churches one sees not statues but only pictures. Yet the pictures are in bold relief, as bas-relief images, and they are held in the most profound reverence.

(3) The Wafer and Bread.

In the service of the mass unleavened bread (the wafer) is used in the Roman churches, while common bread is distributed in the Greek communion. As a protest against Jewish observance of the seventh day, the practice of fasting on Saturday arose in the West but never in the East. Later, the Roman Catholic fast-day was changed to Friday, the day of our Lord's crucifixion. **(4) Fast Day**

But deeper than these differences of ceremony, in bringing about the separation of the Latin and Greek churches, was the political cause in the independence of Europe from the throne of Constantinople, in the establishment of the Holy Roman Empire (800 A. D.). Even after the fall of the old Empire of Rome in 476 A. D. the imperial idea still held power; and the new barbarian kingdoms of the Goths, Franks and other races, in a loose way regarded themselves as theoretically under the emperor at Constantinople. But when the Holy Roman Empire was established by Charlemagne, it took the place of the ancient empire, separate from and independent of the emperors of Constantinople. An independent state necessitated an independent church. **3. Political Cause of Separation.**

But the most powerful force leading to the separation was the persistent claim of Rome to be the ruling church, and of its pope to be the "Universal Bishop." At Rome the church was gradually dominating the state; at Constantinople the church was obsequious to the state. Hence a schism between the two sections with such opposite conceptions was inevitable; and the final rending apart of the two great divisions of the church came, as we have seen, in 1054 A. D. **4. Claims of Rome.**

CHAPTER XV.

THE MEDIEVAL CHURCH.

PART FOUR.

THE CRUSADES.

V. The
Crusades,
1095-1270
A. D.

1. Their
Origin.

Another great movement in the Middle Ages, under the inspiration and at the command of the church, was the crusades, beginning at the end of the eleventh century and continuing for nearly three hundred years. From the fourth century onward even unto the present time pilgrimages have been made by multitudes every year to the Holy Land. The number of the pilgrims vastly increased about the year 1000 A. D. when the end of the world and the coming of Christ were almost universally expected; and even after those events failed to take place, the pilgrimages continued. At first, they were favored by the Moslem rulers of Palestine, but, later, the pilgrims suffered oppression, robbery, and sometimes death. At the same time the weakening eastern empire was menaced by the Mohammedans, and the Emperor Alexis besought Pope Urban II to bring the warriors of Europe to its relief. The spirit arose throughout Europe to free the Holy Land from Mohammedan control, and out of this impulse came the crusades.

The principal crusades were seven in number, besides many other expeditions of lesser importance to which the name was given.   The First Crusade was proclaimed by Pope Urban II in 1095, at the Council of Clermont, where a multitude of knights assumed the cross as a badge, and enlisted for the war against the Saracens.   Before the regular expedition was fully organized, a monk called Peter the Hermit called together an undisciplined multitude, said to number 40,000, and led them toward the East, expecting miraculous aid.   His unorganized, unprovided mob went to failure, many of its members to slavery and death.*   But the first real crusade was undertaken by 275,000 of the best warriors from every land of Europe, led by Godfrey of Bouillon and other chiefs.   After many reverses, chiefly from lack of discipline and dissensions among the leaders, they finally succeeded in taking the city of Jerusalem and nearly all Palestine, in 1099. They established a kingdom on feudal principles, and as Godfrey refused the name of king, he was made "Baron and Defender of the Holy Sepulchre." On Godfrey's death his brother Baldwin took the title of king; and the kingdom of Jerusalem lasted until 1187, though constantly in a precarious condition, because surrounded by the Saracen empire on all sides except the sea, and far distant from its natural allies in Europe.

The Second Crusade was called forth by the news that the Saracens were conquering the outlying

1. The Seven Crusades.

(1) First Crusade, 1095-1099.

Peter the Hermit.

Godfrey of Bouillon.

(2) Second Crusade, 1147-1149.

---

* The story of Peter the Hermit's crusade rests upon no certain authority and is doubted by recent historians.

provinces of the kingdom of Jerusalem, and menacing the city itself. Under the preaching of the saintly Bernard of Clairvaux, Louis VII of France and Conrad III of Germany, led a great army to succor the holy places. They met with many defeats, but finally reached the city; could not regain the lost territory, but did postpone for a generation the final fall of the kingdom.

Louis VII (France). Conrad III (Emp.).

In 1187 Jerusalem was retaken by the Saracens under Saladin, and the kingdom of Jerusalem came to an end, although the empty title "King of Jerusalem" was continued long afterward.

(3) Third Crusade, 1189-1191.

The fall of the city aroused Europe to the Third Crusade (1189–1191) which was led by three prominent sovereigns, Frederick Barbarossa of Germany, Philip Augustus of France, and Richard I "the Lion-hearted" of England. But Frederick, the best general and statesman, was drowned, and the two remaining kings quarreled, Philip Augustus went home, and all the courage of Richard did not avail to bring his army to Jerusalem. But he obtained a treaty with Saladin, by which the Christian pilgrims gained the right to visit the Holy Sepulchre unmolested.

Frederick Emperor. Philip Augustus, France. Richard I, England.

The Fourth Crusade (1201–1204) was worse than a failure, for it wrought in the end great harm to the Christian Church. The Crusaders were turned aside from their aim of winning the Holy Land, made war on Constantinople, captured and plundered it, and set up their own rule over the Greek Empire, which lasted fifty years, and left that empire helpless as a bulwark against the growing power of the Turks;

(4) Fourth Crusade, 1201-1204.

Constantinople Taken.

a warlike, uncivilized race, who succeeded the Saracens as the dominant Mohammedan power soon after the close of the crusading period.

In the Fifth Crusade (1228) the Emperor Frederick II, although excommunicated by the pope, led an army to Palestine, and obtained a treaty whereby Jerusalem, Jaffa, Bethlehem and Nazareth were ceded to the Christians; and (as no Roman ecclesiastic would crown him, being under the pope's ban) Frederick crowned himself king of Jerusalem. From that fact the title "King of Jerusalem" was held by all the German emperors, and afterward by the emperors of Austria until 1835. But through the quarrel between the pope and emperor the results of the crusade were lost; Jerusalem was retaken by the Mohammedans in 1244; and since has remained under their control.* (5) Fifth Crusade, 1228, 1229. Frederick II, Emperor.

The Sixth Crusade (1248–1254) was undertaken by Louis IX of France, known as St. Louis. He made his invasion by way of Egypt, and though at first successful, was defeated and taken prisoner by the Mohammedans. At an immense price he was ransomed, and went on to Palestine, remaining there until 1252 when the death of his mother, whom he had left as regent, compelled him to return to France. (6) Sixth Crusade, 1248-1254. St. Louis.

The Seventh Crusade (1270–1272) was also under the leadership of St. Louis, jointly with Prince Edward Plantagenet of England, afterward King Edward I. The route chosen was again by way of Africa; but Louis died at Tunis, his son made peace, (7) Seventh Crusade, 1270-1272. St. Louis, Prince Edward, England.

* On December 8, 1917, the city of Jerusalem was surrendered to the British army, and on December 11th, the British general in command entered the city and took formal possession in the name of his government, and of the allied powers.

and Edward returned to England to become king; so this, generally regarded as the last of the crusades, came to naught.

There were minor crusades, so called, but none deserving special mention. In fact, from 1270 onward any war undertaken even nominally in behalf of the church was called a crusade, even when against "heretics" in Christian countries.

3. Causes of Failure of the Crusades.

(1) Dissensions of Leaders.

The Crusaders failed to free the Holy Land from the dominion of the Mohammedans; and, looking back over the period, we can readily see the reasons for their failure. One fact will be noted in the story of every crusade: the kings and princes who led the movement were perpetually quarreling, each chieftain caring more for his own interests than for the common cause; all jealous of one another, and fearful of a success which might promote the influence or fame of a rival. Against their divided, suspicious, half-hearted effort was arrayed a fearless, united people, a race always bold in war, and under the absolute rule of one commander, whether caliph or sultan.

(2) Limited Views.

But a deeper cause of failure was the unstatesmanlike views of these leaders. They possessed no large, far-sighted vision. Immediate results were all that they looked for. They did not realize that to found and maintain a kingdom in Palestine, a thousand miles from their own lands, required constant communication with western Europe, a strong base of supply, continual reinforcement. The conquest of the land was an intrusion, not a liberation. The people of Palestine were practically enslaved by the

Crusaders; as slaves were compelled to build castles, fortresses, and palaces for their hated masters; and they welcomed the return of their former Moslem rulers, for heavy as their yoke had been, it was lighter than that of the Christian kings of Jerusalem.

Yet, despite the failure to maintain a Christian kingdom in Palestine, certain good results came to Europe from the crusades. After the crusades the pilgrims were protected by the Turkish government, and persecution ceased. In fact, the land became more prosperous, and the cities of Bethlehem, Nazareth, and Jerusalem increased in population and in wealth, through the tide of pilgrims sweeping over Palestine, under guarantees of safety from the Turkish rulers.

4. Some Good Results of the Crusades.
(1) Pilgrims Protected.

After the crusades, Moslem aggressions on Europe were checked. The experience of those centuries awakened Europe to the danger from Islam. The Spaniards were encouraged to make war upon the Moors, who held half of the peninsula. Under Ferdinand and Isabella, the Spaniards, in 1492, subjugated the Moorish kingdom, and expelled the Mohammedans from the land. On the eastern frontier of Europe, Poland and Austria stood on guard, and in 1683 turned back the tide of Turkish invasion in a great battle won near the city of Vienna. This victory marked the beginning of decline in the power of the Turkish Empire.

(2) Moslem Aggressions Checked.
In the West.

In the East.

Another result of the crusades was a better acquaintance of nations with each other. Not only the rulers and chieftains, but the inferior

(3) Aquaintance among Nations.

knights and even the soldiers of the different lands began to know each other, to recognize interests in common. Among nations a mutual respect for each other arose, and alliances were formed. The crusades were a great contribution toward the development of modern Europe.

(4) Impulse to Trade.

The crusades furnished a great impulse to trade. The demand for supplies of every kind—arms, provisions, guides, ships—promoted manufactures and commerce. The Crusaders brought home a knowledge of the wealth in the Orient, its carpets, silks, jewels, and a trade in these arose all over western Europe. Merchants grew rich; a middle class arose between lord and serf; the cities advanced in power, and the castles began to decline in their control over them. In the after centuries, the cities became the centers of freedom and reform, breaking away from the arbitrary control of both princes and prelates.

(5) Power of the Church.

The ecclesiastical power was at first greatly increased through the crusades. The wars were waged at the call of the church, which thereby showed its domination over princes and nations. Moreover, the church bought lands, or loaned money on them as security to crusading knights, and greatly enlarged its holdings throughout Europe. And in the absence of temporal rulers, bishops and popes gained control. But in the final result, the vast wealth, the overweening ambition, and the unscrupulous use of power by churchmen, aroused discontent, and aided to pave the way for the approaching revolt against the Roman Catholic Church in the Reformation.

CHAPTER XVI.

THE MEDIEVAL CHURCH.

PART FIVE.

DEVELOPMENT OF MONASTICISM. MEDIEVAL ART
AND LITERATURE.

We have already noted the origin of the monastic life in the caves of upper Egypt, during the fourth century. In Europe the movement was at first of slow growth, but the Middle Ages showed a great development of the monastic spirit, both among men and women. The number of monks and nuns increased enormously, with results both good and evil.

VI. Development of Monasticism.

In the East the early ascetics lived apart, each in his own cave or hut, or upon his pillar, but in western Europe they formed communities, dwelling together. As these settlements grew in size and in number, some form of organization and government became necessary, and in process of time four great orders arose.

1. Monastic Orders.

The earliest of these orders was the Benedictines, founded by St. Benedict in 529 A. D. at Monte Cassino, in the Apennines, midway between Rome and Naples. This order became greatest of the monastic communities of Europe, and in its earlier stage promoted the Christianization and civiliza-

(1) Benedictines, 529 A. D. St. Benedict.

tion of the North. Its rules required obedience to the head of the monastery, poverty or the possession of no property by the individual monk or nun, and personal chastity. This order was active in industrial works. They cut down the forests, drained the swamps, tilled the fields, and taught the people many useful arts. Many of the later orders were branches or outgrowths from the Benedictines.

(2) Cistercians, 1098. St. Robert. St. Bernard.

The Cistercians arose in 1098, aiming to strengthen the Benedictine discipline, which had grown somewhat lax. Their name came from Citeaux, in France, where the order was founded by St. Robert; but in 1112 it was strengthened and reorganized by the saintly Bernard of Clairvaux. This order gave great attention to art, architecture, and especially to literature, copying ancient books and writing many new ones.

(3) Franciscans, 1209. St. Francis.

The Franciscans were founded in 1209 by St. Francis of Assisi, one of the holiest, most devoted, and most lovable of men. From Italy they spread rapidly over all Europe and became the most numerous of all the orders. It is said that in the Black Death, the pestilence which swept through Europe in the fourteenth century, more than 124,000 of the Franciscan monks perished while ministering to the dying and the dead. From the color of their habit they became known as the Grey Friars.

(4) Dominicans, 1215. St. Dominic.

The Dominicans were a Spanish order, founded by St. Dominic in 1215, and extending into all the countries of Europe. These differed from the other orders in being preachers, going everywhere to strengthen the faith of believers and oppose the growing tendencies to "heresy," of which in later times they were the fiercest persecutors. They were known as the Black Friars from their garb. These, with the Franciscans, were also called "Mendicant Friars," because they depended for their support upon alms which they collected from door to door. Beside these were similar orders for women.

All these ascetic orders began with the noblest aims, and were founded by self-sacrificing men and women. Their influence was partly for good, partly for evil. At first, during the earlier period of each monastic order, it was a benefit to society. Let us recognize some of the good results of monasticism.

Through ages of war, almost of anarchy, there were centers of peace and quiet in the monasteries, where many in trouble found refuge. The monasteries gave hospitality to travelers, the sick, and the poor. Both the modern hotel and the modern hospital grew out of the hospice or monastery. Often the monastery or the convent was a refuge and protection to the helpless, especially to women and children. The early monasteries both in Great Britain and on the continent promoted agriculture by the example of the monks in drainage, control of water-courses, the building of roads, and instruction in cultivating the soil. In the libraries of the monasteries were preserved many of the ancient works in literature, both classical and Christian. The monks copied books, wrote lives of distinguished men, chronicles of their own time, and histories of the past. Many of the most precious religious works, such as the songs of St. Bernard and The

2. Benefits of Monasticism.

(1) Centers of Peace.

(2) Hospitality.

(3) Refuge.

(4) Agriculture.

(5) Literature.

Imitation of Christ by à Kempis, have been given to the world by the monasteries. Without their historical writings, the Middle Ages would be a blank indeed. In the education of youth the monks were the principal teachers, almost the only teachers; nearly all the universities and schools of the Middle Ages arose in the abbeys and monasteries.

(6) Education.

In the diffusion of the gospel the monks were the early missionaries. They met the incoming barbarians and converted them to Christianity. Of these St. Augustine (not the great theologian) who came from Rome to England (597 A. D.) and St. Patrick, who began the evangelization of Ireland in 440 A. D. were examples among many monastic missionaries.

(7) Missions.

But if these good results flowed from the monastic system, there were also evil results. Some of these evils were apparent even when the institution was at its best, but they grew more manifest in the later periods, when monasticism degenerated, lost its early fervor, its lofty aims, and its strict discipline. Among these evils were the following:

2. Some Evil Results of Monasticism.

Monasticism set forth the celibate life as the higher life, which is unnatural and unscriptural. It enforced the monastic life upon untold thousands of the noblest men and women of their age. Homes were established and families reared, not by the best men and women, but by those of lower ideals. It secluded multitudes not only from family life, but also from social, civic, and national life. Alike in peace and in war, good men who were needed in the state, were idle in the monasteries.

(1) Exaltation of Celibacy.

(2) Effects on Social and National Life.

It has been asserted that Constantinople and the Eastern Empire could have been defended from the Turks if monks and ecclesiastics had taken up weapons and fought for their country. The growing wealth of the monasteries led to lax discipline, to luxury, to idleness, to open immorality. Many of the convents became sinks of iniquity. Each new order was an effort for reform, but its members eventually dropped down to the lower levels of conduct. Originally the monasteries were supported by the labor of their occupants; but in the later ages their work almost entirely ceased, and the monks and nuns were maintained by the revenues of their constantly increasing property, and by contributions extorted from families, rich and poor. All real estate owned by the monastic houses was exempt from taxation. Thus an increasing and finally insupportable burden was laid upon society outside the convents. Their rapacity led to their extinction.

(3) Luxury and Immorality.

(4) Contributions Extorted.

At the opening of the Reformation in the sixteenth century, the monasteries everywhere in northern Europe had fallen so low in the estimation of the people that they were universally suppressed, and those dwelling within their walls were compelled to labor for their support.

It was formerly the custom to call this period "the Dark Ages"; yet those centuries gave to the world some of the greatest achievements in the finer things of life; and all these were wrought under the direct influence of the church.

VII. Medieval Art and Literature.

During the Middle Ages arose nearly all the great universities, established mainly by churchmen, and

1. Universities.

growing out of earlier schools connected with the cathedrals and monasteries. Among these are to be named the University of Paris, which, in the eleventh century, under Abelard, embraced 30,000 students; the universities of Oxford and Cambridge, and of Bologna—to which students journeyed from **2. Cathedrals.** all European lands. All the great cathedrals of Europe—those marvels of Gothic architecture—upon which the modern world looks, but which it cannot hope to surpass or even to equal—were planned and built during the medieval period. The awakening of literature began in Italy, with Dante's Divine Comedy, which was begun about 1303, and soon followed by the writings of Petrarch (1340) and Boccaccio (1360).

In the same land, and about the same time, began the awakening of art with Giotto, in 1298, followed by a series of great painters, sculptors and architects. It is to be remembered that almost without exception the early painters used their art for the service of the church; and their works, though now in picture galleries, were originally in the churches and monasteries.

CHAPTER XVII.

THE MEDIEVAL CHURCH.

PART SIX.

BEGINNINGS OF RELIGIOUS REFORM. THE FALL OF CONSTANTINOPLE. SCHOLARS AND LEADERS.

During this period, and especially toward its close, gleams of religious light began to shoot over the age, foretokens of the coming Reformation. Five great movements for reform in the church arose; but the world was not ready for them, and they were repressed with bloody persecution.

VIII. Beginnings of Religious Reform.

The Albigenses or Cathari, "puritans," grew up to prominence in southern France, about 1170. They repudiated the authority of tradition, circulated the New Testament, and opposed the Romish doctrines of purgatory, image-worship, and priestly claims; although they held some peculiar views allied to the ancient Manicheans, and rejected the Old Testament. Pope Innocent III, in 1208, called for a "crusade" against them, and the sect was extirpated by the slaughter of almost the entire population of the region, Catholic as well as heretic.

1. Albigenses, 1170.

The Waldensians were founded about the same time, 1170, by Peter Waldo, a merchant of Lyons, who read, explained, preached and circulated the

2. Waldensians, 1170.

Scriptures, to which he appealed against the usages and doctrines of the Roman Catholics. He established an order of evangelists, "The Poor Men of Lyons," who went through central and southern France, gaining followers. They were bitterly persecuted; but, driven out of France, found hiding places in the valleys of northern Italy, and in the face of centuries of persecution have endured, and constitute a part of the comparatively small group of Protestants in Italy.

3. John Wyclif, 1324-1384. John Wyclif began the movement in England for freedom from the Roman power and for reformation in the church. He was born in 1324, and was educated at the University of Oxford, where he became doctor of theology, and the leading spirit in its councils. He attacked the mendicant friars, and the system of monasticism; rejected and opposed the authority of the pope in England; wrote against the doctrine of transubstantiation, i. e., that in the mass the bread and wine are transformed into the veritable body and blood of Christ; regarding them merely as symbols, and urged that the church service be made more simple, according to the New Testament pattern. In other lands he would have suffered martyrdom, but in England he was protected by the most powerful among the nobles; and though some of his doctrines were condemned by the University, he was allowed to retire to his parish at Lutterworth and remain undisturbed as a priest. His greatest work was his translation of the New Testament into English, finished in 1380; the Old Testament, in which he was aided by friends, appearing in 1384, the year of Wyclif's death. His followers were called Lollards, at one time numerous, but under kings Henry IV and Henry V persecuted and finally extinguished. Wyclif's preaching and his translation prepared the way for the Reformation.

John Huss, in Bohemia (born 1369, martyred 1415), was a reader of Wyclif's writings, and preached his doctrines, especially proclaiming freedom from papal authority. He was made rector of the University of Prague, and for a time held a commanding influence throughout Bohemia. The pope excommunicated him, and laid the city of Prague under an interdict while he remained there. Huss retired, but from his hiding-place sent forth letters reaffirming his views. After two years he consented to go before the Council of the Roman Catholic Church at Constance, in Baden on the border of Switzerland, having received a safe conduct from the Emperor Sigismund. But the pledge was violated, upon the principle that "faith was not to be kept with heretics." Huss was condemned and burned to death in 1416, but his fate aroused the reforming element in his native land, and has influenced Bohemia through all the centuries since his day.

4. John Huss, 1369-1415.

Jerome Savonarola (born 1452) was a monk of the Dominican order at Florence in Italy, and Prior of the Monastery of St. Mark. He preached, like one of the old prophets, against the social, ecclesiastical, and political evils of his day, filled the great cathedral to overflowing with multitudes eager not only to listen, but to obey his teachings. For a time he

5. Jerome Savonarola, 1452-1498.

was the practical dictator of Florence, and effected a seeming reformation. But he was excommunicated by the pope, was imprisoned, condemned, hanged, and his body burned, in the great square of Florence. His martyrdom was in 1498, only nineteen years before Luther nailed his theses on the cathedral door at Wittenberg.

IX. Fall of Constantinople, 1453.

The fall of Constantinople in 1453 has been fixed upon by historians as the dividing point between medieval and modern times. The Greek Empire never recovered from the conquest of Constantinople by the Crusaders in 1204; but the strong defenses, natural and artificial, long protected the city against the Turks, who succeeded the Arabians as the leading Mohammedan power. Province after province of the great empire was shorn away, until only the city of Constantinople was left, and, in 1453, it was finally taken by the Turks under Mohammed the Second. In one day the church of St. Sophia was transformed into a mosque, and Constantinople became, as it remained until 1920, the city of the Sultans and the capital of the Turkish Empire. Angora (Ankara) became the Turkish capital in 1923. The Greek Church continues with its patriarch, shorn of all but ecclesiastical authority, residing in Constantinople (Istanbul). With the fall of Constantinople, 1453, ends the period of the Medieval Church.

X. Scholars and Leaders.

Let us mention very briefly some of the scholars and leaders of thought in the period which we have studied. During the thousand years of the Medieval Church many great men arose, but we name only four of them as the intellectural leaders of their age.

Anselm was born 1033 in Piedmont in Italy, and at first, like many others, a wandering scholar in various lands, but became a monk at the Monastery of Bec in Normandy, and was made abbot in 1078. He was appointed by William Rufus Archbishop of Canterbury and Primate of the Church of England, in 1093; but strove against William and his successor Henry I, for the liberty and authority of the church, and for a time suffered banishment. He was the writer of many theological and philosophical works, and has been called "a second Augustine." He died in 1109.

1. Anselm, 1033-1109.

Peter Abelard, born 1079, died 1142, as philosopher and theologian, was the boldest thinker of the Middle Ages. He may be regarded as the founder of the University of Paris, which was the mother of the European universities. His fame as a teacher drew students by the ten thousand from every part of Europe, and many of the great men in the generation succeeding his own were influenced by his thought. His daring speculations and independent opinions more than once brought him under the ban of the church. Even more famous than his teachings and writings has been the romantic story of his love-affair with the beautiful Heloise for whom he broke his monastic vows. They were married, but afterward compelled to separate. Both entered convents; Abelard died an abbot and Heloise an abbess.

2. Abelard, 1079-1142.

Bernard of Clairvaux (1091–1153) came of a noble French family. He was educated for the

3. Bernard of Clairvaux, 1091-1153.

court, but renounced it for the convent. In 1115 he established at Clairvaux a monastery of the reformed Cistercian order, and became its first abbot. His branch of the order took root in many countries, and its members were commonly known as Bernardines. Bernard was a remarkable union of the mystic and the practical thinker. He preached and promoted the Second Crusade in 1147. A broad-minded gentle-hearted man, he opposed and wrote against the persecution of the Jews. Some of his hymns, as "Jesus, the very thought of Thee," and "O Sacred Head, now wounded," are sung in all the churches. Only twenty years after his death he was canonized as St. Bernard. Luther said "If there ever lived on earth a God-fearing and holy monk, it was St. Bernard of Clairvaux."

4. Thomas Aquinas, ?226-1274. The greatest mind of the Middle Ages was that of Thomas Aquinas, who lived 1226 to 1274, and was called "Universal Doctor," "Angelical Doctor," and "Prince of Scholastics." He was born at Aquino in the kingdom of Naples; and, against the will of his family, the counts of Aquino, entered the Dominican order of monks. While a young student he was so silent as to be nicknamed "the dumb ox;" but his master, Albertus Magnus, said "This ox will one day fill the world with his bellowing." He became the most celebrated and highest authority of all the medieval period in philosophy and theology, and his writings are still often quoted, especially by Roman Catholic scholars. He died in 1274, and was canonized as a saint in 1323.

OUTLINE OF CHAPTERS XVIII, XIX, XX.

FIFTH GENERAL PERIOD. THE REFORMED CHURCH.

From the Fall of Constantinople, 1453 A. D.,
To the End of the Thirty Years' War, 1648 A. D.

I. ANTECEDENT FORCES LEADING TO THE REFORMATION (CHAPTER XVIII).

1. The Renaissance.
2. The Invention of Printing.
3. The Spirit of Nationality.

II. THE REFORMATION IN GERMANY (CHAPTER XVIII).

1. The Sale of Indulgences.
2. The Theses.
3. Burning the Papal Bull.
4. The Diet of Worms.
5. The Wartburg.
6. The Protestant Name.

III. THE REFORMATION IN OTHER LANDS (CHAPTER XIX).

1. In Switzerland.
2. On the Scandinavian Kingdom.
3. In France.
4. In the Netherlands.
5. In England.
    (1) Under Henry VIII.
    (2) Under Edward VI.
    (3) Under Queen Mary.
    (4) Under Queen Elizabeth.
6. In Scotland.

IV. THE PRINCIPLES OF THE REFORMED RELIGION (CHAPTER XIX).

1. Scriptural Religion.
2. Rational Religion.
3. Personal Religion.
4. Spiritual Religion.
5. National Religion.

V. THE COUNTER-REFORMATION (CHAPTER XX).

1. Reform within the Roman Catholic Church.
2. The Order of Jesuits.
3. Active Persecution.
4. Missionary Efforts of Roman Catholics.
5. The Thirty Years' War.

VI. LEADERS OF THE PERIOD (CHAPTER XX).

1. Desiderius Erasmus, 1466-1536.
2. Martin Luther, 1483-1546.
3. John Calvin, 1509-1564.
4. Thomas Cranmer, 1489-1556.
5. John Knox, 1505-1572.
6. Ignatius Loyola, 1491-1556.
7. Francis Xavier 1506-1552.

WORKS FOR FURTHER STUDY.

Cowan.   Landmarks of Church History, Chaps. XXII-XXVI.
Selden.   Story of the Christian Centuries, Chaps. V, VI, VII.
Zenos.   Compendium of Church History, pp. 198-266.
Sohm.   Outlines of Church History, pp. 146-187.
Moncrief.   Short History of the Christian Church, pp. 279-369.
J. H. Blunt.   Key to the Knowledge of Modern Church History.
Epochs of Church History.   The Protestant Reformation.   Williston
Walker.
Fisher.   History of the Christian Church, pp. 287-393.
Hurst.   History of the Christian Church, Vol. II, pp. 3-565.
Schaff.   History of the Christian Church, Vols. VI, VII.
Mrs. E. R. Charles.   The Diary of the Schonberg-Cotta Family.
(Fiction.)
Thomas Carlyle in Heroes and Hero-Worship.   Martin Luther.
T. B. Macaulay's Essay on Von Ranke's History of the Popes.

CHAPTER XVIII.

THE REFORMED CHURCH.

FROM THE FALL OF CONSTANTINOPLE, 1453 A. D., TO
THE END OF THE THIRTY YEARS' WAR, 1648.

PART ONE.

THE REFORMATION IN GERMANY.

In this period of two hundred years, the great fact which arrests attention is the Reformation, which began in Germany and spread over all northern Europe, resulting in the establishment of national churches owning no allegiance to Rome. Let us notice some antecedent forces leading to the Reformation, and greatly furthering its progress. *The Reformation. I. Antecedent Forces.*

One of these forces was that remarkable movement known as the Renaissance, or the awakening of Europe to a new interest in literature, art and science; the change from medieval to modern aims and methods of thought. During the Middle Ages the interest of scholars had been in religious truth, with philosophy as related to religion; and the chief thinkers and writers, as we have seen, were churchmen. But in this awakening a new interest arose in classic literature, Greek and Latin, in art, *1. The Renaissance.*

soon drawing apart from religion, and with that interest came the first gleams of modern science. The leaders of the movement were generally not priests nor monks, but laymen, especially in Italy, where the Renaissance began, not as a religious but a literary movement, yet not openly anti-religious, so much as skeptical or enquiring. Most of the Italian students of the period were men devoid of religious life; even the popes of that time were marked by culture, rather than faith. North of the Alps, in Germany, England and France, the movement was more religious, awakening a new interest in the Scriptures, Greek and Hebrew, and a search for the true foundations of faith, apart from the dogmas of Rome. Everywhere, South and North alike, the Renaissance undermined the Roman Catholic Church.

In Italy, Literary.

In the North. Religious.

The invention of printing called forth a herald and ally of the coming reform, in the press. The discovery was made by Gutenberg, in 1455, at Mayence on the Rhine, that books could be printed from movable types, and with ease disseminated by the thousand. Before this invention, from the beginning of time, books had been circulated only as rapidly as they could be copied out by hand. A Bible in the Middle Ages cost the wages of a working man for a year. It is significant as showing the desire of that time, that the first book printed by Gutenberg was the Bible. The press brought the Scriptures into common use, and led to their translation and circulation in all the languages of Europe. The people who read the New Testament soon

2. The Invention of Printing. Gutenberg, 1455.

realized that the papal church was far from the New Testament ideal. And the new teachings of the Reformers, as fast as they appeared, were set forth in books and pamphlets, which were circulated by the million throughout Europe.

There was also arising in Europe a spirit of nationality. This differed from the medieval strifes between emperors and popes, in that it was more a popular than a kingly movement. The patriotism of the people was beginning to manifest itself in an unwillingness to submit to a foreign rule over their own national churches; to resist the appointment by a pope in a distant land, of bishops abbots, and church dignitaries; a disposition to withhold the contribution of "Peter's pence" for the support of the pope and the building of stately churches in Rome; and a determination to abridge the power of the church councils, bringing the clergy under the same laws and courts with the laity. This national spirit was a strong support to the reforming movement. **3. The Spirit of Nationality.**

While the spirit of reform and of independence was awakening through all Europe, the flame burst forth first in Germany, in the electorate of Saxony, under the leadership of Martin Luther, a monk and professor in the University of Wittenberg. Let us notice some of its earlier stages. **II. The Reformation in Germany.** **Martin Luther**

The reigning pope, Leo X, needing large sums of money for the completion of St. Peter's Church at Rome, permitted an agent named John Tetzel to go through Germany selling certificates, signed by the pope himself, purporting to bestow the pardon of **1. The Sale of Indulgences.**

all sins, not only upon the holders of the certificates, but upon friends living or dead in whose behalf they were purchased, without confession, repentance, penance, or absolution by a priest. Tetzel told the people "As soon as your coin clinks in the chest, the souls of your friends will rise out of purgatory to heaven." Luther preached against Tetzel and his selling of pardons, denouncing his teaching in no measured terms.

2. Luther's Theses, 1517. The exact date fixed upon by historians as the beginning of the Great Reformation, is October 31, 1517. On the morning of that day Martin Luther nailed to the oaken door of Wittenberg Cathedral a parchment containing ninety-five theses or statements, nearly all relating to the sale of indulgences, but in their application striking at the authority of the pope and the priesthood. The rulers of the church vainly endeavored to coerce and to cajole Luther, but he stood firm, and the storm only made him more resolute in his opposition to doctrines and practices not countenanced by Holy Scripture.

3. Burning the Papal Bull, 1520. After many controversies, and the publication of pamphlets which made Luther's opinions known throughout Germany, his teachings were formally condemned, and he was excommunicated by a bull* of Pope Leo X in June, 1520. The Elector Frederick of Saxony was commanded to deliver up Luther for trial and punishment, but, instead, he gave him ample protection, as he sympathized with his views. Luther met the excommunication with

---

*The decrees of a pope are called "bulls," from the Latin word *bulla*, "a seal;" the name being applied to any document stamped with an official seal.

defiance, called it "the execrable bull of Antichrist," and on December 10, 1520, publicly burned it at the gates of Wittenberg, before an assemblage of the University professors, the students, and the people. With the papal bull he burned also copies of the canons or laws enacted by the Roman authorities. This act constituted Luther's final renunciation of the Roman Catholic Church.

In 1521, Luther was summoned before the Diet or Supreme Council of the German rulers, meeting at Worms on the Rhine. The new emperor, Charles the Fifth, gave him the promise of a safe conduct, and Luther went to the assembly, though warned by his friends that he might meet the fate of John Huss in similar circumstances at the Council of Constance, in 1415. Luther said "I will go to Worms, though as many devils were aiming at me as tiles on the roof." On April 17, 1521, Luther stood before the Diet, over which the emperor was presiding, and in answer to the question whether he would retract the statements in his books, replied, after consideration, that he could retract nothing except what was disproved by Scripture or reason, ending with the words: "Here I stand; I can do naught else. God help me. Amen." The Emperor Charles was urged to seize Luther, on the ground that no faith was to be kept with heretics, but he permitted him to leave Worms in peace. *4. The Diet at Worms, 1521.*

While Luther was traveling homeward, he was suddenly arrested by soldiers of the Elector Frederic, and taken, for his safety, to the castle of the Wartburg in Thuringia. He remained there nearly *5. The Wartburg Castle.*

a year, in disguise, while storms of war and revolt were raging in the empire. But he was not idle, for during this retirement he made his translation of the New Testament into the German tongue, a work which alone would have made him immortal, for his version is regarded as the Foundation of the German written language. This was in 1521; the Old Testament was not completed until several years later. Coming from the Wartburg back to Wittenberg, he resumed his leadership in the movement for a Reformed Church, just in time to save it from extravagant excesses.

Luther's Bible.

The division of the German states into the reformed and Roman branches was between the North and South. The Southern princes, led by Austria, adhered to Rome, while those of the North were mainly followers of Luther. A Diet was held at Spires in 1529, in the vain hope of reconciling the two parties. At this Diet, the Catholic rulers were in the majority, and condemned the Lutheran doctrines. The princes forbade any teaching of Lutheranism in states where it had not become dominant; and in the states already Lutheran required that the Catholics should be allowed the free exercise of their religion. To this unequal ruling the Lutheran princes made a formal protest, and from that time they were known as Protestants, and their doctrines as the Protestant religion.

6. The Protestant Name. Diet of Spires, 1529.

CHAPTER XIX.

THE REFORMED CHURCH.

PART TWO.

THE REFORMATION IN OTHER LANDS. THE PRINCIPLES OF THE REFORMATION.

While the Reformation was in its earliest stages in Germany, the same spirit broke out in many other lands of Europe. In the South, as Italy and Spain, it was put down with a relentless hand; in France and the Netherlands the cause of reform hung in the balance of uncertainty; but among all the northern nations the new religion was victorious over all opposition and ruled the lands. **II. The Reformation in Other Lands.**

The Reformation in Switzerland arose independently of that in Germany, though simultaneous with it; under the leadership of Ulric Zwingli, who, in 1517, attacked the "remission of sins" through pilgrimages to a shrine of the Virgin at Einsieldn; and in 1522 definitely broke from Rome. The Reformation was formally organized at Zurich, and soon became more radical than in Germany; but its progress was hindered by a civil war between the Roman Catholic and Protestant cantons, in in which Zwingli was slain in 1531. The reform went onward, however, and found its later leader in John Calvin, the greatest theologian of the **1. In Switzerland, Zwingli.**

John Calvin.

(155)

church after Augustine; whose "Institutes of Theology," published in 1536, when Calvin was only twenty-seven years old, became the standards of Protestant doctrine.

2. Denmark, Sweden, Norway. The Scandinavian kingdom, comprising at that time Denmark, Sweden, and Norway under one government, early received Luther's teachings which were favored by King Christian II. Political strife and civil war for a time interfered with the progress of the Reformation, but in the end all the three lands accepted the Lutheran views.

3. France. In France, the Roman Catholic Church possessed greater liberty than in the rest of Europe, and hence there was less demand for ecclesiastical independence from Rome. But a religious movement arose among the French people, even earlier than in Germany, for, in 1512, Jacques Lefevre wrote and preached the doctrine of "Justification by faith." **Lefevre, 1512.** Two parties appeared in the court and among the people, and successive kings, all nominally Roman Catholic, sided at one time or another with each party. But Protestantism received almost a death-blow in the terrible massacre of St. Bartholomew's Day, August 24, 1572, when nearly all its leaders and countless thousands of their followers were murdered. In the face of persecution the reformed faith lived, and a minority of the French people have been Protestant. Though small in numbers, French Protestantism has been great in its influence.

4. The Netherlands. The Netherlands, comprising what are now the two kingdoms of Holland and Belgium, were at the beginning of the Reformation period under the dominion of Spain. They received the reformed teachings early, but were bitterly persecuted by the Spanish regents. In the Low Countries the reform was a demand for political as well as religious liberty, and the tyranny of Spain drove the people to revolt. After a long war and incredible suffering, the Netherlands, under the leadership of William the Silent, at last obtained independence from Spain, although it was not recognized until 1609, twenty-five years after his death. Holland on the north became Protestant, but Belgium remained mainly Roman Catholic.

The movement for the Reformation in England **5. In England.** passed through various stages of advance and retrogression, from its political relations, from the differing attitude of the successive sovereigns, and from the conservatism of the English nature. It began in the reign of Henry VIII with a band of **(1) Under Henry VIII.** young students in classical literature and the Bible; some of whom, like Sir Thomas More, paused in their progress and remained Catholic, while others pressed on boldly to the Protestant faith. One of the leaders in the English Reformation was John Tyndale, who translated the New Testament into his **John Tyndale Martyred, 1536.** mother-tongue, the earliest version in English after the invention of printing, and the one which more than any other has shaped all the translations since. Tyndale was martyred at Antwerp in 1536. Another leader was Thomas Cranmer, Archbishop **Thomas Cranmer.** of Canterbury, who, after aiding to make England Protestant, recanted under the Romanist Queen Mary, in the hope of saving his life, but when condemned to die by fire, recalled his recantation. The reform was both helped and hindered by King Henry VIII, who broke from Rome because the pope would not sanction his divorce from Queen Katharine, the sister of the emperor, Charles V; and established an English Catholic Church with himself as its head. Henry VIII put to death Romanists and Protestants alike who differed from his views.

(2) Under Edward VI, 1547-1553.

Under Edward VI, a mere youth, whose reign was short, the cause of reform made great progress. Led by Cranmer and others, the Church of England was established, and the Prayer Book compiled in its rich and rhythmic form of speech.

(3) Under Queen Mary, 1553-1558.

Queen Mary, who followed Edward VI, was a bigoted Romanist, and undertook to bring her subjects back to the old church by lighting the fires of persecution. She reigned only five years, but in that time more than three hundred Protestants suffered martyrdom.

(4) Under Queen Elizabeth, 1558-1603.

With the accession of Elizabeth, the ablest of all the sovereigns of England, the prisons were opened, the exiles were recalled, the Bible again stood in honor in the pulpit and in the home, and during her long reign, which has given its name, "Elizabethan," to the most glorious age in English history, the Church of England was re-established and took the form in which it has continued to the present day.

5. In Scotland.

The Reformation at first made slow advance in Scotland, where the church and state were ruled with iron hand by Cardinal Beaton and the Queen-regent, Mary of Guise, the mother of Mary Queen of Scots. The cardinal was murdered, the Queen-regent died, and soon afterward John Knox, in 1559, assumed the leadership of the reforming movement. By his radical and uncompromising views, his unbending determination, and his resistless energy, even against the opposition of the abilities and fascinations of his Romanist sovereign Mary Queen of Scots, he was able to sweep away every vestige of the old religion, and to carry the reform far beyond that in England. The Presbyterian Church as planned by Knox became the established church of Scotland. *John Knox, 1505-1572.*

At the opening of the sixteenth century, the only church in western Europe was the Roman Catholic, apparently secure in the loyalty of every kingdom. Before the end of that century every land of northern Europe west of Russia, had broken away from Rome and had established its own national church.

While in the lands of northern Europe there were differences in doctrine and in organizations the result of the Reformation, yet it is not difficult to find the common platform of all the Protestant churches. The principles of the Reformation may be named as five in number.* *IV. Principles of the Reformation.*

The first great principle is that true religion is founded upon the Scriptures. The Roman Catholics had substituted the authority of the church for that of the Bible. They taught that the church was infallible, and the authority of the Bible proceeded *1. Scriptural Religion.*

*On this subject the outline and much of the material is taken from "Landmarks of Church History," by Henry Cowan, D.D.

from its authorization by the church. They withheld the Scriptures from the laity, and strongly opposed every translation of them into the language spoken by the common people. The reformers declared that the Bible contained the standards of faith and practice; and that no doctrine was to be accepted unless it was taught in the Bible. The Reformation brought a lost Bible back to the people, and placed its teachings upon the throne of authority. It is through the Reformers and mainly in Protestant lands, that the Bible is now circulated by many million copies annually.

2. Rational Religion. Another principle established by the Reformation was that religion should be rational and intelligent. Romanism had introduced irrational doctrines like transubstantiation into the church's creed, preposterous pretensions like papal indulgence into her discipline, superstitious usages like image-worship into her ritual. The reformers, while duly subordinating reason to revelation, recognized the former as a divine gift, and demanded a creed, a discipline, and a worship, which should not outrage man's rational nature.*

3. Personal Religion. A third great truth made emphatic in the Reformation was that of personal religion. Under the Roman system a closed gate stood between the worshiper and God, and to that gate the priest held the only key. The repentant sinner did not confess his sins to God, but to the priest; he did not obtain forgiveness from God, but from the priest, who alone could pronounce absolution. The worshiper did

*Cowan, page 168.

LUTHER'S THESES NAILED TO THE CHURCH DOOR, 1517

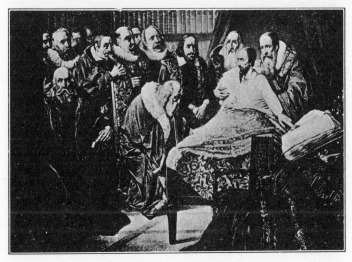

CALVIN'S LAST INTERVIEW

MARTIN LUTHER

not pray to God the Father through Christ the Son, but through a patron saint, who was supposed to intercede for him with a God too high for man in this earthly life to approach. In fact, God was looked upon as an unfriendly Being, who must be appeased and placated by the ascetic lives of saintly men and women whose prayers alone could avail to save men from God's wrath. The godly-minded could not go for guidance to the Bible, but must take its teachings at second-hand, as interpreted by the councils and canons of the church. All these barriers the reformers swept aside. They pointed the worshiper to God as the direct object of prayer, the immediate giver of pardon and of grace. They brought each soul into the presence of God and the fellowship of Christ.

The Reformers also insisted upon a spiritual as against a formal religion. The Roman Catholics had overloaded the simplicity of the gospel with a mass of forms and ceremonies which completely obscured its life and spirit. Religion consisted in external services rendered under priestly direction, and not in the attitude of the heart toward God. Undoubtedly there were many earnest, spiritual natures in the Roman Catholic Church, men like Bernard of Clairvaux, Francis of Assisi, and Thomas à Kempis, living in intimate communion with God. But throughout the church in general, religion was of the letter and not of the spirit. The Reformers emphasized the inward rather than the outward traits of religion. They brought forth the ancient doctrine as a vital experience, "salvation by faith

4. Spiritual Religion.

in Christ and by faith only." They proclaimed that men are righteous, not by outward forms and observances, but by the inward spiritual life, "the life of God in the souls of men."

5. National Religion.

The last of these principles in the practical working of the Reformation was that of a national church as distinct from one universal. The aim of the papacy and the priesthood had been to subordinate the state to the church, and to make the pope supreme over all nations. Wherever Protestantism triumphed a national church arose, self-governed, and independent of Rome. These national churches assumed different forms, Episcopal in England, Presbyterian in Scotland and in Switzerland, somewhat mixed in northern lands. The worship in every Roman Catholic Church was and still is in Latin, but every Protestant Church maintains its services in the language spoken by the worshipers.

CHAPTER XX.

THE REFORMED CHURCH.

PART THREE.

THE COUNTER-REFORMATION. LEADERS OF THE PERIOD.

Not long after the Reformation began, a mighty effort was made by the Roman Catholic Church to regain its lost ground in Europe, to subvert the Protestant faith, and to promote Roman Catholic missions in foreign lands. This movement is called the Counter-Reformation.

V. The Counter-Reformation.

Reform within the church was attempted through the Council of Trent, called in 1545 by Pope Paul III, mainly to investigate and put an end to abuses which had called forth the Reformation. The council met at different times, and in more than one place, though mainly at Trent in Austria, seventy-six miles northwest of Venice. It was composed of all the bishops and abbots of the church, and lasted nearly twenty years, through the reigns of four popes, from 1545 to 1563. The hope had been that the chasm between Catholics and Protestants might be bridged over, and Christianity reunited; but this could not be accomplished. Yet many reforms were made, the doctrines of the church were definitely stated, and even Protestants admit that the popes since the

1. Church Reform. Council of Trent, 1545-1563.

Council of Trent have been better men than many of those before it. The result of the council might be considered a conservative reformation within the Roman Catholic Church.

2. Order of Jesuits, 1534.
A more powerful influence in the Counter-Reformation was the Order of Jesuits, established in 1534, by a Spaniard, Ignatius Loyola. This was a monastic order characterized by the union of the strictest discipline, the most intense loyalty to the church and the order, the deepest religious devotion, and a strong proselyting endeavor. Its principal aim was to fight the Protestant movement with methods both open and secret; and it became so powerful as to incur the bitterest opposition, even in Roman Catholic countries; was suppressed in nearly every state of Europe, and by decree of Pope Clement XIV, 1773, forbidden throughout the church. But it was continued for a time in secret, afterward openly, was again recognized by the popes, and is now one of the most potent forces for the spreading and strengthening of the Roman Catholic Church throughout the world.

3. Active Persecution.
Active persecution was another weapon employed to quell the growing spirit of reform. It is true that Protestants also persecuted, even to death; but generally their motive was political, rather than religious. In England, those put to death were mainly Catholics who conspired against Queen Elizabeth. But on the continent every Roman Catholic government sought by fire and sword to extirpate the Protestant faith. In Spain, the Inquisition was established and untold multitudes were

tortured and burned.   In the Low Countries, the Spanish rulers undertook to kill every one suspected of heresy.   In France, the persecuting spirit reached its height in the massacre on St. Bartholomew's Day, and for weeks afterward, in 1572, when by different estimates from twenty thousand to one hundred thousand people perished.   These persecutions in every land where Protestantism was not in control of the government, not only stayed the reforming tide, but in some countries, notably Bohemia and Spain, crushed it out.

The missionary efforts of the Catholic church must be recognized as one of the forces in the Counter-Reformation.   This was largely, though not entirely, under the direction of the Jesuits.   It resulted in the conversion of all the native races of South America and Mexico, and in a large part of Canada;   and in the establishment of great missions in India and the lands adjoining by the saintly Francis Xavier, one of the original founders of the Jesuit society.   Roman Catholic missions in heathen lands began centuries earlier than Protestant missions, and have greatly increased the numbers and power of the church. **4. Catholic Missions.**

As the inevitable effect of the clashing interests and aims of the Reformed and Catholic states in Germany, a war began in 1618, a century after the opening of the Reformation, and finally involved nearly all the European nations.   It is known in history as the Thirty Years' War.   Political rivalries as well as religious became involved, and states of the same faith were at times on opposing sides. **5. Thirty Years' War. 1618-1648.**

For nearly a generation the strife went on, and all Germany suffered inconceivably. Finally, in 1648, the great war was ended by the Peace of Westphalia, which fixed the boundaries of Roman Catholic and Protestant states mainly as they have continued unto the present time. At that point, therefore, the Period of the Reformation may be considered as ended.

VI. Leaders of the Period. In an epoch so momentous, embracing so many lands, and fraught with such far-reaching results, there were of necessity many leaders on both the Reformed and Catholic sides. Only a few of these can be named in our brief account of the movement.

1. Desiderius Erasmus, 1466-1536. Desiderius Erasmus, born in Rotterdam, Holland, 1466, was one of the greatest scholars of the Renaissance and Reformation period. He was trained in a monastery and ordained, but left the priesthood about 1492, and devoted himself to literature. At different times he lived in Paris, England, Switzerland, and Italy, but his home was mainly at Basle, in Switzerland. Before the Reformation opened, he became a relentless critic of the Roman Catholic Church, in many writings, of which the most widely circulated was his "Praise of Folly." His greatest and most valuable work was his edition of the New Testament in Greek, with a Latin translation. Although Erasmus accomplished as much as any man of his age in preparing for the Reformation, yet he never joined the movement, remained outwardly a Catholic and criticised .the Reformers as sharply as he did the old church. He died in 1536.

Unquestionably the foremost figure in the period was Martin Luther, "the founder of Protestant civilization." He was born at Eisleben, in 1483, the son of a miner, who, by great effort, sent him to the University of Erfurt. Luther aimed to be a lawyer, but suddenly felt the call of duty to become a monk, and entered the Augustinian monastery. He was ordained to the priesthood, and soon attracted notice by his ability; was sent to Rome in 1511, and was disenchanted by what he saw there of the worldliness and wickedness in the church. In 1511, he began his career as a reformer by attacking the selling of "indulgences," or pardons for sins, and as we have seen nailed his theses to the door of the church in Wittenberg. When excommunicated, cited to Rome, and in his absence, condemned by Pope Leo X, he burned the pope's bull or decree, in 1520. He made his celebrated response at the Diet of Worms, April 18, 1521. While returning home, in danger of assassination by his enemies, he was seized by his friends, and hidden for nearly a year in the Wartburg Castle; employing his seclusion in the translation into German of the New Testament. Returning to Wittenberg, he became again the leader in the Reformation. In 1529 an effort was made to unite the followers of Luther and Zwingli, but it was unsuccessful, on account of Luther's unwavering, uncompromising spirit. He was the author of many writings, which circulated throughout Germany, but most influential of all was his matchless translation of the Bible. He died while on a visit to his birthplace, Eisleben, February 18, 1546, at the age of sixty-three.

2. Martin Luther, 1483-1546.

3. John Calvin, 1509-1564.

John Calvin, the greatest theologian in Christendom since St. Augustine, Bishop of Hippo, was born at Noyon, France, July 10, 1509, and died at Geneva, Switzerland, May 27, 1564. He studied at Paris, Orleans, and Bourges, embraced the Reformed teachings in 1528, and was banished from Paris. In 1536 he published at Basel his "Institutes of the Christian Religion," which became the basis of the doctrine of all the Protestant churches except the Lutheran. In 1536 he fled to Geneva, where he lived, with an interruption of a few years of banishment, until his death. His Protestant Academy, which he founded with Theodore Beza and other Reformers, became one of the principal centers of Protestantism in Europe. The Calvinistic theology and the Lutheran theology possess rational and radical traits, which have inspired the liberal movements of modern times, in both state and church, and have contributed mightily to the progress of democracy throughout the world.

4. Thomas Cranmer, 1489-1556.

Thomas Cranmer may be regarded as the leader of the English Reformation, from his position as the first Protestant at the head of the English Church. While a young man he fell under the favorable notice of King Henry VIII through his suggestion of an appeal to the universities of Europe on the question of the king's divorce. He served Henry VIII on various embassies, and was made Archbishop of Canterbury. Although progressive in his views, he was also timid and pliable, wielding his influence for moderate rather than radical measures of reform in the church. During the minority of King

Edward VI he was one of the regents, and was able to advance the cause of Protestantism. Cranmer's greatest service was as one of the compilers of the Prayer Book, and writer of nearly all the articles of religion. On the accession of Queen Mary, he was deposed from his archbishopric, and committed to prison. Under stress of suffering he recanted his Protestant opinions in hope of saving his life, but was condemned to die by burning. Before his martyrdom, in 1556, he renounced his disavowal, and died bravely, holding out in the fire his right hand which had signed his recantation, that it might be the first to burn.

John Knox was the founder of the Scottish Church, and has been rightly called "the father of Scotland." He was born in or near 1505, in the Lowlands, was educated at the University of St. Andrews for the priesthood, and ordained, but instead of entering upon the pastorate became a teacher. Not until he was forty-two years old, about 1547, did he embrace the cause of reform. He was made prisoner with other Reformers by the French allies of the Queen-regent, and sent to France, where he served in the galleys, but was released, and spent some years as an exile partly in England under King Edward VI, and after the accession of Queen Mary, on the Continent. At Geneva he met John Calvin, and adopted his views both in doctrine and in church government. In 1559 he returned to Scotland, and became at once the leader, almost the absolute ruler, in the Reformation of that land. He was able to make the Presbyterian faith and order

5. John Knox, 1505-1572.

supreme in Scotland, and to direct a reform more radical than in any other land of Europe. He died in 1572. As his body was lowered into its grave, Morton, the regent of Scotland, pointed to it with the words. "There lies a man who never feared!"

6. Ignatius of Loyola, 1491 (1495?)-1556.

Among the great men of this great period, at least two should be named of those eminent on the Roman Catholic side. One of these was Ignatius of Loyola, a Spaniard, born either in 1491 or 1495, of a noble family, in the Castle of Loyola, from which he took his name. Up to the age of twenty-six he was a brave, though dissolute soldier; but after a severe wound and a long illness he devoted himself to the service of the church, and in 1534 established the Society of Jesus, generally known as the Jesuits, the most powerful institution of modern times for the promotion of the Roman Catholic church. His writings were very few, the constitutions of the order, which have been practically unchanged to the present time; his letters, and "Spiritual Exercises," a small work, but one that has greatly influenced not only the Jesuits, but all the Catholic religious orders. Ignatius of Loyola must be recognized as one of the most remarkable and most influential personalities in the sixteenth century. He died in Rome, July 31, 1556, and was canonized as a saint in 1622.

7. St. Francis Xavier, 1506-1552.

Saint Francis Xavier (who well deserved his title) was born in 1506 in the Spanish section of Navarre, at that time an independent kingdom on both sides of the Pyrenees. He was one of the original members of the Jesuit society, and took for his department of its work that of foreign missions, of which he became the modern founder. He established the Roman Catholic faith in India, in the island of Ceylon, in Japan, and in other lands of the Far East. He was just beginning a work in China, when he died suddenly of a fever, in 1552, at the age of only forty-six years. During his short life he brought about the conversion of pagans numbering many thousands; and he organized his missions so wisely that the Christianizing movement went on after his death. As the result of his labors and plans the Roman Catholics in the East now include many millions. Throughout his life Xavier showed a gentle, broad-minded, generous spirit which has endeared his memory to Protestants as well as to Catholics.

OUTLINE OF CHAPTERS XXI, XXII.

SIXTH GENERAL PERIOD. THE MODERN CHURCH.

From the End of the Thirty Years' War, 1648,
To the Twentieth Century, 1901.

I. THE PURITAN MOVEMENT (CHAPTER XXI).

1. Its Origin.
2. Its Divisions.
3. Its Supremacy.
4. Its Results.

II. THE WESLEYAN REVIVAL (CHAPTER XXI).

1. The Need.
2. The Leaders.
3. Growth of the Movement.
4. Relation to the Church.
5. Its Results.

III. THE RATIONALISTIC MOVEMENT (CHAPTER XXI).

1. Its Origin.
2. Its Growth.
3. Its Decline.
4. Its Effects.

IV. THE ANGLO-CATHOLIC MOVEMENT (CHAPTER XXI).

1. Names.
2. Aim.
3. Beginning.
4. Leaders.
5. Tendency.
6. Results.

V. THE MODERN MISSIONARY MOVEMENT (CHAPTER XXII)

1. Missions in the Early Church.
2. Neglected in the Later Medieval and Reformation Periods.
3. Moravian Foreign Missions.
4. English Foreign Missions.
5. American Foreign Missions.
6. Present Missionary Conditions.

VI. LEADERS OF THE MODERN PERIOD (CHAPTER XXII).

1. Richard Hooker, 1553-1600.
2. Thomas Cartwright, 1535-1603.
3. Jonathan Edwards, 1703-1758.
4. John Wesley, 1703-1791.
5. John Henry Newman, 1801-1890.
6. William Carey, 1761-1834.

**VII. THE CHURCH IN THE TWENTIETH CENTURY
(CHAPTER XXII).**

1. Doctrine.
2. Unity of Spirit.
3. Spirit of Service.

WORKS FOR FURTHER STUDY.

Cowan. Landmarks of Church History, Appendix.
Selden. Story of the Christian Centuries, Chap. VIII.
Zenos. Compendium of Church History, pp. 247-334.
Sohm. Outline of Church History, pp. 188-254.
Moncrief. Short History of the Christian Church, pp. 370-467.
Epochs of Church History—The Anglican Reformation. William Clark.
Fisher. History of the Christian Church, pp. 484-664.
Hurst. History of the Christian Church, Vol. II, pp. 573-918.
Macaulay's Essays on John Milton and John Bunyan.
S. P. Cadman. Three Religious Leaders of Oxford.
C. T. Winchester. Life of John Wesley.
W. H. Fitchett. Wesley and His Century.
J. H. Overton. The Anglican Revival.
R. W. Church. The Oxford Movement.
E. M. Bliss. A Concise History of Missions.

CHAPTER XXI.

THE MODERN CHURCH.

PART ONE.

THE PURITAN MOVEMENT. THE WESLEYAN
REVIVAL. THE RATIONALISTIC MOVE-
MENT. THE ANGLO-CATHOLIC
MOVEMENT.

In our study of the modern **period**, the last two
centuries and a half-century, our attention will be
directed mainly to the churches which arose out of
the Reformation. The Roman Catholic Church has
pursued its own way, entirely apart from the Protestant world; and is outside our horizon. Our
aim will be to sketch very briefly certain important
movements which, since the Reformation, have influenced the lands mainly Protestant, as England,
North Germany, and America. I. The
Puritan
Movement.

Soon after the Reformation three distinct parties
appeared in the English Church; the Romanizing
element, seeking friendliness and reunion with
Rome; the Anglican, satisfied with the moderate
reforms accomplished under King Henry VIII and
Queen Elizabeth; and the radical Protestant party,
aiming for a church similar to those established in
Geneva and in Scotland. This latter party became
known about 1654 as "the Puritans," and so strongly
1. Its Origin.

opposed the Anglican system under Queen Elizabeth, that many of its leaders were driven into exile. The

2. Its Divisions.

Puritans also had their division into two elements, those favoring the Presbyterian form, and the more radical element seeking the independence of each local society, known as "Independents" or "Congregationalists." As yet, however, all these parties remained as members of the English Church.

3. Its Supremacy.

In the strife between Charles I and the Parliament, the Puritans were strong champions of popular rights. At first the Presbyterian wing became dominant, and under the order of Parliament, an assembly of Puritan ministers held at Westminster, in 1643, prepared the Westminster Confession of Faith, and the two catechisms, long regarded as the Presbyterian and Congregational standards. During Oliver Cromwell's rule (1653–1658) the Independent or Congregational element triumphed. With Charles II (1659–1685) the Anglicans again assumed power, and the Puritans were persecuted

4. Its Results.

as Non-conformists. After the Revolution of 1688, they were recognized as Dissenters from the Church of England, and obtained rights as separate organizations, entirely outside the Establishment. Out of the Puritan movement arose three churches, the Presbyterian, the Congregational, and the Baptist.

II. The Wesleyan Revival.

1. The Need.

In the first half of the eighteenth century, the churches in England, both Established and Dissenting, sank into a state of decline, with formal services, cold, intellectual belief, and a lack of moral power over the population. From this condition England was awakened by a group of earnest

preachers led by the brothers John and Charles
Wesley and George Whitefield. Of these, Whitefield was the greater pulpit orator, stirring the
hearts of untold thousands both in England and
America; Charles Wesley was the sacred poet,
whose hymns have enriched every collection since
his day; but John Wesley was the unquestioned
leader and statesman of the movement. At the age
of thirty-five, an Anglican clergyman, John Wesley
found the reality of a spiritual religion among the
Moravians, a body of Dissenters from the Lutheran
Church. In 1739 he began preaching "the witness
of the Spirit" as a personal consciousness, and
formed societies of those who accepted his teachings.
At first these societies were conducted by class-
leaders, but later Wesley called forth a body of lay-
preachers, who carried his doctrines and their experience to every part of Great Britain, and to the
American colonies. His followers were early nicknamed "Methodists," and Wesley accepted the
name. In England they became known as "Wesleyan Methodists," and before his death numbered
many thousands.

Although for many years violently opposed in the
Church of England, and shut out of its pulpits,
Wesley always declared himself its loyal member,
regarding his society not as a separate denomination but an organization within the English Church.
Nevertheless, after the American Revolution in
1784, he organized the Methodists in the United
States, numbering at that time 14,000, into a separate church according to the Episcopal plan, and gave

2. The
Leaders.

3. Growth
of the
Movement.

4. Relation
to the
Church.

them "superintendents," a title which he preferred to "bishop;" but in America, the name "bishop" was soon preferred and became general.

5. Its Results.

The Wesleyan movement awakened the Christian life among Churchmen and Dissenters to new power. It also led to the formation of Methodist churches under varied forms of organization in many lands. On the American continent, at the opening of the twentieth century, the enrolled membership of Methodists was more than six millions. No single leader in Christian history has obtained so large a personal following as John Wesley.

III. The Rationalistic Movement.

1. Its Origin.

The Reformation established the right of private judgment regarding religion and the Bible, independent of priestly or churchly authority. An inevitable result came to pass, that while some leaders of thought accepted the old views of the Bible as a supernatural book, others began to regard reason as the supreme authority, and to demand a rational and not a supernatural interpretation of Scripture. Those scholars who followed reason as against the supernatural, were termed "rationalists." The germs of rationalism existed in England and in Germany from the beginning of the eighteenth century, but its activity as a distinct movement in the church began with Johann Semler (born 1725, died 1791), who claimed that nothing received from tradition was to be accepted without proof, that the Bible was to be judged by the same criticism as that applied to other ancient writings, that all accounts of miracles were to be discredited, and that Jesus was only a man and not a divine Being.

The rationalistic spirit grew until nearly all the universities of Germany were controlled by it; and it reached its culmination in the publication of Friedrich Strauss' "Life of Jesus," in 1835, undertaking to show that the gospel accounts were "myths" or legends. This work was translated by George Eliot (Marian Evans) in 1846, and obtained a wide circulation in England and America. The three leaders who in the nineteenth century turned the current of thought from rationalistic to orthodox channels were Schliermacher (1768–1834), who has been rightly called "the greatest divine of the nineteenth century," Neander (1789–1850), and Tholuck (1790–1877). Rationalistic scholarship awakened a new spirit of investigation, called forth many strong theologians and Bible interpreters in defense of the truth, and thereby caused the contents of the Bible and the doctrines of Christianity to be widely studied and more intelligently understood. For example, the life of Christ had never been written in a scholarly way until the publication of Strauss' book in 1835; now the intelligent, thoughtful works on the subject may be counted by the thousand. Rationalism, which threatened the overthrow of Christianity, in its effect has developed its strength.

When the nineteenth century was ending the first third of its years, a spirit was awakened in the Church of England, which aroused strong controversy, and in its varied aspects received different names. From its aim, it was called "the Anglo-Catholic movement;" from the university in which it arose it was named "the Oxford movement;"

2. Its Growth.

3. Its Decline.

4. Its Effects.

IV. The Anglo-Catholic Movement.

1. Names.

from its promotion through the publication of ninety numbered tracts by different writers setting forth its views it received the name "Tractarian," and from one of its leading exponents it was frequently spoken of, especially by those who opposed it as "Puseyite" or "Puseyism."

2. Aim. It was an effort to restore the Church of England from Protestantism back to the doctrines and practices of the earlier centuries when the Christian Church was one, and needed no reformation. The leaders in the movement dated its inception from the publication, in 1827, of "The Christian Year," by John Keble, a series of poems which awakened a new interest in the church. The formal beginning,

3. Beginning. however, was a sermon preached by Keble in July, 1833, in St. Mary's, Oxford, on "National Apostacy." Soon afterward a series of remarkable "Tracts for the Times" began to appear, on the polity, doctrines, and worship of the English Church, and continued from 1833 to 1841. While Keble inspired the movement, and was in thorough sympathy with it, its

4. Leaders. leader was John Henry Newman, who wrote many of the Tracts for the Times, and whose sermons from the pulpit of St. Mary's were the popular presentation of the cause. Another of its advocates was the able, scholarly, and deeply religious Canon Edward B. Pusey. Thousands of clergymen and prominent laymen in the Church of England gave their active support to the movement. Great controversies arose; the leaders were denounced as Romanists in spirit and purpose, but the general effect was to strengthen the power and uplift the

standards of the Church. As the spirit of the move- 5 Tendency.
ment was to discredit the Reformation and encour-
age Anglo-Catholicism, it had an inevitable tendency
toward Rome; and in 1845, its great leader, Newman, followed the logic of his convictions into the
Roman Catholic Church. His secession, with that
of others, was a shock, but did not stop the Anglo-
Catholic current. ·

CHAPTER XXII.

THE MODERN CHURCH.

PART TWO.

THE MODERN MISSIONARY MOVEMENT. LEADERS
OF THE MODERN PERIOD. THE CHURCH
IN THE NEW CENTURY.

V. The Modern Missionary Movement.

1. Missions in the Early Church.

For a thousand years from the days of the apostles, Christianity was a working missionary institution. In the first four centuries of its history the church won the Roman Empire from heathenism to Christianity. Afterward, its missionaries met the advancing hordes of barbarians and conquered them

2. Neglected Later.

before they conquered the Western Empire. After the tenth century, church and state, pope and emperor, were in strife for supreme control, and the missionary spirit declined, though it was never entirely lost. The Reformation was concerned with efforts to purify and reorganize the church, rather than to extend it. We have seen that in the later age of the Reformation the first extensive effort to Christianize the heathen world was made, not by Protestants, but by Roman Catholics under St. Francis Xavier.

3. Moravian Missions, 1732.

As early as 1732, the Moravians began to establish foreign missions, by sending Hans Egede to

Greenland, and soon afterward the same church was working among the Indians of North America, the Negroes in the West Indies, and in the oriental lands. In proportion to its small membership at home, no other denomination has maintained as many missions as the Moravian Church throughout its history.

The founder of modern missions from England was William Carey. He had been a shoemaker, was self-educated, and became a Baptist minister in 1789. In the face of strong opposition he began to urge the sending of missionaries to the heathen world. A sermon which he preached in 1792, under the two heads: (1) Attempt great things for God, and (2) Expect great things from God, led to the organization of the Baptist Missionary Society, and the sending of Carey to India. He was not permitted by the English East India Company, then governing India, to land, and found a foothold at Serampore, a Danish colony near Calcutta. Overcoming his lack of early education he became one of the leading scholars of the world in Sanscrit and other oriental languages. His grammars and dictionaries are still used. From 1800 to 1830 he was professor of oriental literature in Fort William College, Calcutta. He died in 1834, revered throughout the world as the father of a great missionary movement.

4. English Missions. William Carey.

The missionary enterprise in America received its first inspiration from the famous "Haystack Prayer Meeting" at Williams College, Massachusetts, in 1811. A group of students met in a field for prayer on the subject of missions. A storm came up; they

5. American Missions. Haystack Meeting.

took refuge under a haystack, and there consecrated their lives to work for Christ in the heathen

American Board.

world. Out of this meeting came the American
Board of Commissioners for Foreign Missions, which
was at first interdenominational, but as other
churches formed societies of their own, soon became
the enterprise of the Congregational churches. The
American Board sent out four missionaries, of whom
two, Newell and Hale, went to India. The others,
Judson and Rice, on their voyage to the Far East,
changed their views regarding baptism, and resigned
from the American Board. Their action resulted in
the formation of the American Baptist Missionary
Society, and Judson and Rice entered upon work
in Burma. The example of the Congregationalists
and Baptists was followed by other denominations,
and before many years each church had its own
board and its own missionaries.

6. Present Missionary Conditions.

At the present time, there is scarcely a land on
earth without the gospel in one form or another.
Christian schools, colleges, hospitals, orphanages
and other philanthropic institutions are found
throughout the heathen world, and the annual
receipts of the various mission boards mount up to
many millions. The most prominent feature in the
church of today, in Great Britain and America, is
its deep and wide-spread interest in foreign missions.

VI. Leaders of the Modern Period.

Out of the many great men who have appeared
in the last three centuries it is difficult to name the
leaders in Christian thought and activity. The
following may be pointed out as representative men
in the movements of their times.

Richard Hooker (1553–1600) was the author of the most famous and influential work on the constitution of the Church of England. Born of poor parents, he obtained aid in his education at Oxford University, where he gained great learning in varied lines, and was made in succession, tutor, fellow, and lecturer. He was ordained in 1582, and for a time was co-pastor in London with an eloquent Puritan, while Hooker was Anglican in his views. Their controversies in the pulpit finally led Hooker to seek a country parish where he could find time for study. His great work was "The Laws of Ecclesiastical Polity," in eight books, the ablest presentation of the episcopal system ever published, and the one from which most writers since his day have drawn their arguments. Yet it is liberal in its attitude toward the non-episcopal churches, and singularly free from a bitter controversial spirit. Hooker was only forty-seven years old at his death.

1. Richard Hooker, 1553-1600.

Thomas Cartwright (1535–1603) may be regarded as the founder of English Puritanism, though not the greatest of its adherents. That honor belongs to Oliver Cromwell, whose record, however, is in the history of the state and not of the church. Cartwright became professor of divinity in Cambridge University in 1569, but lost his position in the following year on account of his published opinions, which were obnoxious to Queen Elizabeth and the leading bishops. He advocated the view that the Scriptures contain not only the rule of faith and doctrine, but of church government; that the church should be Presbyterian in its system; that it should

2. Thomas Cartwright, 1535-1603.

not only be independent of the state, but practically supreme over the state. He was as intolerant as the high churchmen in demanding uniformity in religion, to be enforced by civil authority, provided that the church should be Presbyterian and its doctrine that of John Calvin. For a few years Cartwright was a pastor over the islands of Guernsey and Jersey, where he planted churches of his own persuasion; but from 1573 to 1592, he was most of the time either in prison or in exile on the Continent. The last nine years of his life seem to have been passed in retirement. Later, his views became dominant in the House of Commons, while prelacy ruled in the House of Lords, and the strife between the parties at last culminated in the civil war, and the rule of Cromwell.

3. Jonathan Edwards, 1703-1758.

Jonathan Edwards (1703–1758) ranks as the foremost of all Americans in metaphysics and theology, and the greatest theologian of the eighteenth century on either side of the Atlantic. In him were combined the keenest logic, the utmost ardor in theological enquiry, and a devout spiritual fervor. From his earliest youth he was precocious, was graduated from Yale College at the age of seventeen, having already read widely in the philosophic literature of the past and of his own time. In 1727 he became co-pastor with his grandfather of the Congregational Church in Northampton, and soon became known as an ardent advocate of an earnest spiritual life. From his pulpit went forth "the Great Awakening," a revival which spread through all the American colonies. His opposition to the "half-way covenant" then almost universally accepted in New England—by which persons were admitted to church membership without a definite religious character—aroused a bitter feeling against him, and led to his dismissal from his church in 1750. For eight years he was a missionary to the Indians; and during this period of retirement wrote his monumental work on "The Freedom of the Will," ever since his time the text-book of New England Calvinism. In 1758 he was made president of Princeton College, but after a very few weeks of service, died at the age of fifty-five.

John Wesley was born at Epworth, in the north of England, in the same year with Jonathan Edwards in America, 1703, but outlived him a third of a century until 1791. His father was for forty years rector of the Church of England in Epworth. But John Wesley owed more to his mother, Susanna Annesley Wesley, who was descended from a line of Puritan and non-conformist ministry, and was the mother and the teacher of eighteen children. Wesley was graduated from Christ Church College, Oxford, in 1724, was ordained in the Church of England, and was for some years a fellow of Lincoln College. During his fellowship he became associated with a group of students in Oxford who aimed at holy living, and were spoken of in derision as "the Holy Club," afterward from their manner of life as "Methodists," a name which became fixed in later years upon Wesley's followers. In 1735 Wesley and his younger brother Charles went as missionaries to the new colony of Georgia. Their

4. John Wesley, 1703-1791.

labors could not be considered successful, and they returned to England after two years. But this period in both their lives was mighty in its results, for at that time they met a group of Moravians, followers of Count Zinzendorf, and from them gained the knowledge and conscious experience of a spiritual life. Up to this time the ministry of John Wesley had been a failure, but henceforth no preacher in England, save George Whitefield, aroused everywhere such interest. Wesley traveled on horseback all over England and Ireland, preaching, organizing societies, and directing them throughout a long life, lasting until almost the end of the eighteenth century. Out of his labors arose not only the Wesleyan body in Great Britain, under several forms of organization, but also the Methodist churches of America and throughout the world, in their membership aggregating many millions. He died in 1791 at the age of eighty-eight.

5. John Henry Newman, 1801-1890. John Henry Newman (1801-1890) by the ability and lucid style of his writings, the clearness of his views, the fervency of his preaching, and above all by a peculiar personal charm, was the leader in the Anglo-Catholic movement of the nineteenth century. He received his degree from Trinity College, Oxford, in 1820, and became a fellow at Oriel College, with the highest honors, in 1824; was ordained in the English Church and in 1828 became vicar of St. Mary's, the University Church, where his sermons enabled him to wield a commanding influence over the men of Oxford for a generation. Although the Oxford movement was begun by John Keble,

its real leader was Newman.   He wrote twenty-nine
of its ninety tracts, and inspired most of the remain-
der.   Partly because the movement was frowned
upon by the authorities in the University and the
leading bishops of the church, but more because his
own views gradually underwent a change, Newman,
in 1843, resigned from St. Mary's, having already
retired to a church at Littlemore, and lived
in seclusion for three years, until 1845, when he
was received into the Roman Catholic Church.
He lived forty-five years after this change of church
relations, most of the time at Birmingham, less
prominent than before, but still beloved by his old
friends.   His writings were many, but the most
widely circulated and influential were his tracts and
several volumes of sermons.   A book which he
published in 1864, entitled *Apologia pro Vita Sua*,
the account of his own religious life and his change
of opinions, showed his absolute sincerity and
increased the reverence already felt toward him
among all except a few bitter partisans.   He was
made a cardinal in 1879, and died in Birmingham
in 1890.   No churchman of any denomination in
his century outranks Newman in his influence.

The story of William Carey (1761–1834), the
founder of modern Protestant missions, has already
been told and need not be repeated.   His monument
is the vast system of missionary preaching and education which is transforming the heathen world.

At the opening of the twentieth century the
Protestant churches of England and America showed
traits very different from those of a hundred years

VII. The
Church in the
Twentieth
Century.

1. Doctrine. ago. Doctrinal systems have dropped into comparative unimportance; and practically all the denominations hold the same creed. The difference between predestination and the freedom of the human will may be held as an academic question but is no longer a practical test. Clergymen now pass from the ministry of one denomination to that of another with no change of belief. Gradually the churches are coming to a unity of the faith.

2. Unity of Spirit. There is a growing unity of spirit corresponding to the unity of belief. Churches no longer stand apart, opposed to each other. They plan together and work together in great movements. The actual union of churches has come about in several instances. Notable illustrations are the United Church of Canada, formed by a union of Methodists, Congregationalists, and part of the Presbyterians in 1925; the union of the Church of Scotland and the United Free Church in 1929; the union of the Congregational and Christian churches in the United States in 1931; and the great union of Methodists in Britain (Primitive, United Methodists, and Wesleyans) in 1932.

3. Spirit of Services. But the most prominent trait in the Christianity of today is its spirit of service. Once the aim was to draw men out of the world into the church; now the aim is to "Christianize the social order," to impart the spirit of the gospel into life in every department.

OUTLINE OF CHAPTERS XXIII, XXIV, XXV

PART ONE. CHAPTER XXIII.

I. THE ROMAN CATHOLIC CHURCH.

1. Spanish Catholics.
2. French Catholics.
3. English Catholics.
4. Catholic Immigration.
5. Catholic Government.

II. PROTESTANT EPISCOPAL CHURCH.

1. In Virginia.
2. In New York.
3. During the American Revolution.
4. Earliest Bishops.
5. Membership.
6. Organization.

III. CONGREGATIONAL CHURCHES.

1. The Pilgrims.
2. Organization.
3. Growth.
4. Doctrines.
5. Membership.

IV. REFORMED CHURCHES.

1. The Reformed Church in America.
2. The Reformed Church in United States.
3. Doctrines.
4. Organization.

V. THE BAPTISTS.

1. Principles.
2. System.
3. Spirit.
4. Origin in Europe.
5. In America.
6. Baptist Bodies.
7. Baptist Missions.

VI. THE FRIENDS OR QUAKERS.

1. George Fox.
2. Quaker Teaching.
3. Quakers in Massachusetts.
4. In New Jersey.
5. William Penn's Colony.
6. Divisions.
7. Membership.

PART TWO. CHAPTER XXIV.

VII. THE LUTHERANS.

1. In New York.
2. On the Delaware River.
3. Growth.
4. Members.
5. Organization.
6. Doctrine.

VIII. THE PRESBYTERIANS.

1. Origin.
2. In the Revolutionary War.
3. Divisions.
4. Membership.
5. Doctrines.
6. Government.

IX. THE METHODISTS.

1. New York and Maryland.
2. Francis Asbury.
3. First Conference.
4. The Christmas Conference.
5. Branches.
6. Members.
7. Doctrines.
8. Organization.

X. THE EVANGELICAL UNITED BRETHREN.

1. Origin.
2. Doctrines.
3. Polity.
4. Division.
5. Members.

XI. THE DISCIPLES OF CHRIST.

1. Origin.
2. Aims.
3. Doctrinal Standards.
4. Ecclesiastical System.
5. Growth.

XII. THE UNITARIANS.

1. Doctrines.
2. Origin.
3. Membership.

XIII. THE CHRISTIAN SCIENTISTS.

1. Its Founder.
2. Organization.
3. Belief.
4. Membership.

XXV. THE CHURCHES IN CANADA.

1. Seventeenth Century Pioneers of Religion.
2. The Catholic Church.
3. Anglican (Church of England).
4. Methodist and Presbyterian.
5. United Church of Canada.
6. Baptist and Lutheran.
7. Doukhobors and Mennonites.
8. Adventists, Brethren, Church of Christ and Disciples of Christ, Christian Science, Evangelical Association, and Others.

CHAPTER XXIII.

THE CHRISTIAN CHURCHES IN THE UNITED STATES.

PART ONE

I. ROMAN CATHOLIC. II. PROTESTANT EPISCOPAL. III. CONGREGATIONAL. IV. REFORMED. V. BAPTIST. VI. SOCIETY OF FRIENDS.

There are in the United States at the present time no less than 265 religious bodies with an estimated 265,500 churches. The inclusive membership of various religious bodies is approximately 89,392,000. Of these, 86,000,000 belong to various Christian denominations.* Only those that appear to be the largest and most important can be noticed, and these very briefly. We take them up in the order of their establishment in America.

As the earliest expeditions to the New World for discovery, conquest, and colonization were from Spain, Portugal and France, all Roman Catholic nations, the first church planted upon the Western Continent, both in South and North America, was the Roman Catholic Church. The history of that church in America begins in the year 1494, when

I. The Roman Catholic Church.

* Statistics on religions can be only very rough approximations. Aside from Christianity, few religions attempt to keep accurate statistical records, and even Catholics and Protestants employ different methods of counting members. All persons of whatever age who have been baptized in the Catholic Church are members, while those in the Protestant Churches must have "joined or been confirmed."

1. Spanish
Catholics.

Columbus, on his second voyage, took with him twelve priests for the conversion of the native races. Wherever the Spaniards went, for settlement or for conquest, they were accompanied by their clergy, who established their religious system. The earliest churches in the United States were at St. Augustine in Florida, in 1565, and in Santa Fé, New Mexico, about 1600. The Spanish method was to enslave the natives, enforce their conversion, and compel then to build churches and monasteries after the plan of those in Spain. Some of their old mission buildings, massive structures, now dismantled and deserted, may still be seen in Texas and California. As the result of the Spanish occupation the territory from Florida to California was, in the eighteenth century, entirely controlled by the Roman Catholic Church. But this vast area was only thinly populated, for the Spaniards, great in conquest, were slow in colonization.

2. French
Catholics.

Soon after the Spanish control of the South, came the French occupation of the North, on the St. Lawrence River, in "New France," or Canada. Quebec was settled in 1608, Montreal not until 1644; and for a time the French immigrants were few. In 1663, the French population of Canada numbered only two thousand five hundred. But soon after, the colonists began coming rapidly, and their birth-rate in America was far above that in France; so that all the region of the St. Lawrence, from the Great Lakes to the Atlantic Ocean, was soon possessed by devoted French Catholics, mainly illiterate, and more submis-

sive to their priests than their fellow Catholics
in France.   In Canada a great effort was made to
win the Indians to the Catholic faith, and history
has no more heroic, self-sacrificing annals than those
of the Jesuits in the French colonies.   Their methods
were in marked contrast with those in Spanish
America.   They won the friendship of the red men
by kindness and unselfish endeavor.

At the middle period of the eighteenth century,
all the territory of the great northwest beyond the
Alleghenies was under French influence; the South-
west was ruled by Spain; and over both possessions
the Roman Catholic Church was supreme, while
only a narrow ribbon along the Atlantic coast was
Protestant under English colonies.   Every forecast
for the future would have pointed to the Catholics
as destined to rule the entire continent.   But the
British conquest of Canada in 1759, and later the
cession of Louisiana and Texas to the United States,
changed the balance of power in North America
from Catholicism to Protestantism.

The English colonies on the Atlantic seaboard **3. English**
were Protestant, except the settlers in Maryland, **Catholics.**
in 1634, who were English Catholics, whose worship
was forbidden in their own country.   Even in the
New World they could obtain a charter only by
allowing freedom to all religions; and soon, the
majority of settlers being Protestants, the Catholic
worship was prohibited, though afterward again
permitted.   Not until 1790 was a Roman Catholic
bishop for Maryland consecrated, the first in the
United States.   At that time the Catholic popula-

tion in this country was estimated at thirty
thousand.

4. Catholic Immigration. A great current of immigration to America from
Europe began about 1845; at first overwhelmingly
Catholic, coming mainly from strongly Catholic
counties in Ireland. To these were added later
other millions from South Germany, and still later
many from Italy. From the natural growth by
birth, from immigration, and a careful priestly
supervision, the Roman Catholic Church in the
United States made great progress until now the
Catholic population is over twenty-eight millions, or
about one third the number of communicants in the
combined Protestant churches.

5. Catholic Government. As a part of the world-wide Roman church, the
American Catholics are under the rule of the pope at
Rome. The nation is divided into one hundred ten
dioceses, each having its bishop appointed by the
pope, to whom nominations are made by the clergy,
which may be accepted or rejected. The dioceses
are united in twenty-four archdioceses, each under an
archbishop; and over all are six cardinal bishops,
also appointed from Rome.

II. Protestant Episcopal Church. The Church of England was the first Protestant
religion established in America. A service was
held under Sir Francis Drake in California, as early
as 1579, and clergymen accompanied the unfortunate
1. In Virginia. expedition of Sir Walter Raleigh in 1587. The permanent entrance of the English Church dates from
1607, with the first English colony at Jamestown,
Virginia. The Church of England was the only
form of worship recognized in the early period in

Virginia and other southern colonies. When New York, settled by the Dutch, became English territory, in 1664, the Church of England was established and soon became the official church of the colony, although other Protestant forms of worship were not forbidden. Trinity parish in New York was constituted in 1693, and Christ Church in Philadelphia in 1695.

2. In New York

Every clergyman of this church was required at his ordination to take an oath of allegiance to the British crown; and as a natural result, nearly all of them were loyalists (called Tories) in the Revolutionary War. Many of the Episcopal clergymen left the country, and at the close of the Revolution it was difficult to supply the vacant parishes, because the requirement of loyalty to Great Britain, could no longer be met; and for the same reason no bishops could be consecrated. In 1784 the Rev. Samuel Seabury, of Connecticut, received consecration from Scottish bishops, who did not require the oath of loyalty, and in 1787, Drs. William White and Samuel Provoost were consecrated by the Archbishop of Canterbury, thus giving to the American Church the English succession. The church in the United States took the official name of the Protestant Episcopal Church. In 1792 the number of its clergymen was about two hundred. The growth of the Episcopal Church since has been rapid and regular. It has now a membership of almost three and one-half millions.

3. During the American Revolution.

4. Earliest Bishops, 1784, 1787.

5. Memberships.

It recognizes three orders in the ministry, bishops, priests, and deacons, and accepts most of the thirty-

6. Organization.

nine articles of the Church of England, modified to fit the American form of government. Its legislative authority is vested in a general convention meeting triennially, in two bodies, a house of bishops, and a house of clerical and lay deputies elected by conventions in the several dioceses.

III. Congregational Churches.

After Virginia with the Church of England, the next region colonized was New England, beginning with the Pilgrims, who landed from the ship Mayflower, at Plymouth, on Massachusetts Bay, in December, 1620. These were "Independents" or "Congregationalists," the more radical element in the English Puritan movement, on account of their views exiled from England to Holland; and now seeking a home in the unoccupied New World.

1. The Pilgrims, 1620.

2. Organization.

Before landing at Plymouth they organized themselves as a pure democracy, with a governor and council elected by popular vote, although under the English flag. They did not at first separate from the Church of England, but regarded themselves as reformers within its pale. According to their convictions, each local church was absolutely independent of outside authority, forming its own platform, calling and ordaining its own minister, and managing its own affairs. Any council or association of churches had only a moral influence, not an ecclesiastical authority, over its several societies. They were in effect a theocracy, and as such all the families in the settlement were taxed for the support of the church, but only members of the church could vote in town and colonial elections. Gradually the restrictions were removed, but not until 1818 in

Connecticut, and 1833 in Massachusetts were church and state absolutely separated and church-support made entirely voluntary.

The persecutions of the Puritans by the rulers of the English Church led multitudes to find refuge and freedom in New England; and the colonies in that region grew more rapidly than elsewhere through the seventeenth century. Two colleges were established, Harvard at Cambridge and Yale at New Haven, both destined to grow into great universities. In general education New England was far in advance of the other colonies in America. As Presbyterians and Congregationalists sprung alike from the Church of England, and both grew Calvinistic in their creeds, accepting the Westminster Confession, the relations of these two bodies were friendly. There was long a tacit understanding, made a formal compact in 1801, that Presbyterian churches should not be formed in New England, nor Congregational churches outside of New England. This, however, was abrogated by a Congregational convention in 1852, and since that time the Congregational system has made rapid progress throughout all the United States, though less in the South than elsewhere. In 1931 the Congregationalists and the Christian Church (General Convention) united at Seattle, Washington, to form the Congregationalist-Christian Church, with a membership of about 1,190,000.

New York was first occupied by the Dutch from Holland as a trading post in 1613, and did not become a town with permanent settlers until 1623.

3. Growth

4. Doctrines.

5. Membership.

IV. Reformed Churches.

1. The
Reformed
Church in
America.

The colony was at first called New Netherlands and the city New Amsterdam. The first church was organized in 1628, under the name of the Reformed Protestant Dutch Church; and during the Dutch supremacy it was the official church of the colony. Churches of this order were established in northern New Jersey, and on both sides of the Hudson River as far as Albany. For more than a hundred years services were held in the Dutch language. In 1664 the colony was taken by Great Britain, renamed New York, and the Church of England became the state religion. But the citizens of Dutch ancestry steadfastly clung to their own church; and its large possessions of property advanced in value with the growth of the city. In 1867 the word "Dutch" was omitted from its official title, which became "The Reformed Church in America." It has many strong churches in the Middle and Far West. The membership is about 184,000.

2. The
Reformed
Church
in U. S.

Another Reformed Church of German origin was brought to this country early in the eighteenth century, and bears the name of "The Reformed Church in the United States." Popularly one church is known as the Dutch Reformed, the other as the German Reformed. A third church of the same order is the Christian Reformed, which grew out of a secession from the state church in Holland, in 1835; and a fourth is "The True Reformed Church." Efforts have been made to unite these four Reformed churches into one organized body,

3. Doctrines.

but thus far without result.

All of these Reformed churches hold to the Calvinistic system of doctrine, teach the Heidelberg Catechism, and are organized upon the same plan, similar to the Presbyterian, but with different names of its ecclesiastical bodies. The ruling board in the local church is the consistory. The neighboring consistories form a classis; the classes of a district are united in a particular synod; and these in a general synod. **4. Organization.**

One of the largest and most widely diffused of the Christian churches in America is the Baptist denomination, numbering in its ten major divisions considerably more than sixteen million members. Their distinctive principles are two: (1) That baptism should be given only to those who profess their faith in Christ, and consequently that infants should not be baptized; (2) That the only Scriptural form of baptism is by the immersion of the body in water, not by sprinkling or pouring. **V. The Baptists.** **1. Principles.**

They are congregational in their system, each local church being absolutely independent of all outside jurisdiction, fixing its own standards of membership and making its own rules. They have no general Confession of Faith, and no catechism for the instruction of the young in their tenets. And yet there is no church in the land more united in its spirit, more active and aggressive in its labors, and more loyal to its principles than are the Baptist churches. **2. System.** **3. Spirit.**

The Baptists arose soon after the opening of the Reformation in Switzerland in 1623, and spread rapidly in North Germany and Holland. They were at first called Anabaptists, because they bap- **4. Origin in Europe.**

tized again those who had already been once baptized in infancy. In England they were at first in union with the Independents or Congregationalists, and gradually became a separate body. In fact, the church at Bedford, over which John Bunyan was pastor about 1660, still in existence, is even now reported as both a Baptist and Congregationalist church.

5. In America.

In America, they began with Roger Williams, a clergyman of the Church of England, who came to New England, and was driven out of Massachusetts because he refused to conform to Congregational rules and opinions. He founded the colony of Rhode Island in 1644*. There all forms of religious worship were free, and enthusiasts of many creeds, persecuted elsewhere, were made welcome. From Rhode Island the Baptists spread rapidly and widely over all parts of the continent.

6. Baptist Bodies.

Of the ten major bodies, the largest are the Southern Baptist Convention, formed in 1845, and now having over seven million members; the National Baptist Convention U.S.A., Inc., with over four million members; the National Baptist Convention, organized in 1895 with a present membership of two and a half million; and the Free Will Baptists, organized in New Hampshire, in 1787, with a membership of over one million five hundred thousand.

7. Baptist Missions.

It will be remembered that the Baptists in England formed the earliest modern missionary society

---

* Some authorities give the date of the First Baptist Church in America as 1639.

in 1792, and sent out William Carey to India. The adoption of Baptist views by Adonirim Judson and Luther Rice, while on the way to Burmah, led to the organization of the Baptist General Missionary Convention in 1814; and since that time the Baptists have been in the forefront of missionary endeavor, and of success.

Of all the movements arising from the great Reformation, the one which swung the farthest away from prelacy and churchly rule, was the Friends, commonly called "the Quakers." This Society—for it never took the name "church"—arose from the teaching of George Fox in England, beginning about 1647. He opposed the outward forms of the church, ritual, and ecclesiastical organization. He taught that baptism and the communion should be spiritual and not formal; that the body of believers should have neither priest nor salaried minister, but that any worshiper should speak as moved by the Spirit of God, who is the "inner light" and guide of all true believers; and that in the gifts of the Spirit and the government of the Society, men and women should have the same privileges. His followers at first called themselves "Children of the Light," but later "The Society of Friends." It is not certain how the name "Quakers" came to be applied to them, but it became general, and is not displeasing to the members of the Society.

VI. The Friends or Quakers.

1. George Fox.

2. Quaker Teaching.

The teachings of George Fox were accepted by multitudes who were out of sympathy with the dogmatic, intolerant spirit at that time manifested by the Church of England. The extent of his influence is shown in the record of nearly fifteen thousand Quakers imprisoned, two hundred transported and sold as slaves, and many dying as martyrs to their faith, either by mob-violence or in prisons. Some sought refuge in New England, but as they brought their testimony, they found the Puritans no less persecuting than the Anglicans. At least four Quakers—one a woman—were executed in Boston.

3. Massachusetts.

The Friends found a safe harbor in Rhode Island, where all forms of faith and worship were free. They formed settlements in New Jersey, Maryland and Virginia. In 1681 the territory of Pennsylvania was given to William Penn, a leader among the Friends, by King Charles II, and Philadelphia, "the Quaker City," was founded in 1682. For seventy years the governors of that colony were descendants of William Penn. In the middle of the eighteenth century, Benjamin Franklin said that the colony was "one-third Quakers, one-third Germans, and one-third miscellaneous."

4. New Jersey.
5. Pennsylvania.

Active persecution ceased both in England and America after the Revolution of 1688 and the Quakers bore their testimony and formed societies in many of the colonies. While their organization was simple, their discipline was strict. Slavery was in existence in every colony but was forbidden among the Friends, and they bore strong testimony against it, even in the southern plantations. They were deeply interested in efforts for the Christianization and civilization of the American Indians, in visiting and aiding prisoners in the wretched jails of that time, and in other philanthropic activities. Many forms of social service now prominent, were initiated and maintained by the Quakers long before they were regarded by others as legitimate church work.

The enforcement of discipline—particularly in the disfellowshiping of members who married outside of the society; the strong testimony against slavery and other evils; and the refusal to bear arms in war, which has ever been one of their principles, caused a decline in the numbers of the Quakers during the eighteenth century. But a greater blow was a 6. Divisions. dissension over the doctrines preached by Elias Hicks, claimed to be Unitarian, not recognizing Christ as God; and in 1827 a separation was made between the Orthodox and Hicksite Friends, although the name "Hicksite" was never sanctioned by that branch. Of these bodies the "Orthodox Friends" as they are called are largely in the majority of membership. Their doctrines are in accord with the churches known as evangelical, with special emphasis upon the immediate personal teaching of the Holy Spirit to the individual, often spoken of as the "Inner Light."

Their present organization is completely democratic. Every person born to Quaker parents is a member, together with those who have been admitted on their own request. All are entitled to take part in the business of the assembly in any meeting in which they are members.

The Five Year Meeting of Friends was formed in

7. Member-ship.

1902, by thirteen yearly meetings. Membership now includes approximately one hundred twelve thousand.

The Society is organized as a series of subordinated meetings which recall to mind the Presbyterian model. Formerly the system was double, the men and women meeting separately for their own appointed business. Recently the meetings have been for the most part held jointly, with equal liberty for all to state their opinions and serve on all committees and other appointments.

In conjunction with good-will centers abroad, the American Society of Friends promotes interest and understanding among oppressed minorities in Europe.

CHAPTER XXIV.

THE CHRISTIAN CHURCHES IN THE UNITED STATES.

PART TWO

VII. LUTHERANS. VIII. PRESBYTERIANS. IX. METHO-
DISTS. X. UNITED BRETHREN. XI. DISCIPLES
OF CHRIST. XII. UNITARIANS. XIII. CHRIS-
TIAN SCIENTISTS.

After the Reformation under Martin Luther, the national churches formed in Germany and the Scandinavian countries took the name of Lutherans. Very early in the history of the Dutch colony of New Amsterdam, afterward New York, some claim as early as 1623, Lutherans, although from Holland, came to that city and held meetings. In 1652 they applied for permission to have a church and pastor; but the Dutch Reformed authorities objected, and caused the first Lutheran minister, in 1657, to be sent back to Holland. The services were continued in a quiet manner, but not until the English conquest of New Amsterdam, in 1664, were the Lutherans allowed freedom of worship. *VII. The Lutherans. 1. In New York.*

In 1638 some Swedish Lutherans settled upon the Delaware, and erected the first Lutheran church in America near Lewes. But the Swedish immigra- *2. On the Delaware River.*

tion soon ceased, and was not renewed until the next century. In 1710 a colony of Lutherans exiled from the Palatinate in Germany brought their church again to New York and Pennsylvania. In the eighteenth century the Protestant Germans and Swedes came to America by the ten thousand, and the first Lutheran Synod was organized at Phila-

3. Growth. delphia in 1748. Since that time the Lutheran churches have grown by immigration and natural increase, until now they number approximately six

4. Members. and a half millions of members.

5. Organization. Coming from different lands and speaking different languages they are organized in at least twelve major independent bodies, some now using English, others still retaining their home-tongues,

6. Doctrine. at least seven in number. In doctrine, they all accept the Augsburg Confession, Luther's doctrine of justification by faith, and a belief that the ordinances of baptism and the Lord's Supper are not mere memorials but channels of divine grace. They are organized into synods, uniting to form a general synod, but reserving much authority to the local churches.

VIII. The Presbyterians. The Presbyterian churches in America sprang from two sources. The earliest was the Presbyte-

1. Origin. rian Church of Scotland, reformed in 1560 by John Knox, and recognized as the established church in that country. From Scotland it spread over into the northwest of Ireland where the population was and still remains Protestant. The other origin was the Puritan movement in England, during the reign of James I; rising to rule in the Parliament in the early period of the Commonwealth.   After the accession of Charles II the Church of England regained its sway, and more than two thousand Puritan pastors, mostly Presbyterian in their views, were ejected from their parishes.   All these three elements, Scotch, Irish and English aided in forming and building up the Presbyterian Church in America.   In New England the Presbyterian immigrants in large part united with the Congregational churches, but in the other colonies they organized churches of their own order.   One of the earliest Presbyterian churches in America was formed at Snow Hill, Maryland, in 1684 by the Rev. Francis Makemie from Ireland.   Makemie and six other ministers met in Philadelphia in 1705, and united their churches into a presbytery.   In 1716, the churches and ministers, having increased in number and extended in their territory, they were organized as a synod, divided into four presbyteries, including seventeen churches.   At the opening of the Revolutionary War, in 1775, the synod included seventeen presbyteries and one hundred and seventy ministers.   The Presbyterians were strong supporters of the rights of the colonies as against George III, and one of their leading ministers, John Witherspoon, was the only clerical signer of the Declaration of Independence.   After the war, the church had grown to such numbers that a General Assembly was formed in Philadelphia, embracing four synods.

2. In the Revolutionary War.

As the Presbyterian principles, as well as the Scotch-Irish nature, tended to strong and inde-

3. Divisions.

pendent thinking upon doctrinal questions, divisions arose in the synods and presbyteries. One of these resulted in the organization of the Cumberland Presbyterian Church, 1810, in Tennessee, from which state it spread to other neighboring states, and even as far as Texas and Missouri. The efforts to reunite this branch with the parent body were, in 1906, successful in large part. In 1837, a division was made over questions of doctrine between two elements, known respectively as the Old and New School Presbyterians, and each had presbyteries, synods, and a General Assembly, claiming to represent *the* Presbyterian Church. After more than forty years of separation, when the difference of views had been forgotten, the two schools were united in 1869. At the opening of the war, in 1861, the Presbyterian churches in the South formed their own church, the Presbyterian Church in the U.S., whereas the church in the North is known as the Presbyterian Church in the U.S.A.

4. Membership.

5. Doctrines.

6. Government.

There are in all ten major branches of Presbyterianism in the United States, with over three million members. All hold substantially to the Calvinistic doctrines, as set forth in the Westminster Confession of Faith, and the Larger and Shorter Catechisms. The local church is governed by a board called the session, composed of the pastor and elders. The churches are united in a presbytery, and the presbyteries in a synod, which generally, but not invariably, follows state lines. Over all is a General Assembly, meeting every year; but important changes in government or doctrine require a ratification by a constitutional majority of the presbyteries and approval by the General Assembly in order to become law.

The Methodist churches in the New World date from the year 1766, when two Wesleyan local preachers, both natives of Ireland, came to America and began holding Methodist meetings. It is uncertain whether Philip Embury held the first service at his own house in New York, or Robert Strawbridge in Frederick County, Maryland. Both of these men formed societies, and in 1768 Philip Embury built a chapel on John Street, where a Methodist Episcopal church still stands. The number of Methodists in America grew, and in 1769, John Wesley sent over two missionaries, Richard Boardman and Thomas Pilmoor, to supervise and extend the work. Other preachers, seven in all, were sent from England later, of whom the most important was Francis Asbury, who came in 1771. The first Methodist Conference in the colonies was held in 1773, Thomas Rankin presiding. But with the opening of the Revolutionary War, all except Asbury left the country, and much of the time, until peace came in 1783, he was in retirement. When the United States were recognized by Great Britain the Methodists in America numbered about fifteen thousand. As they were nominally connected with the Church of England, Wesley endeavored to induce the Bishop of London to consecrate a bishop for America; and, finding his efforts of no avail, he set apart the Rev. Thomas Coke, D.D., a clergyman of the English Church, as "Superintendent"

IX. Methodists.

1. New York and Maryland.

2. Francis Asbury.

3. First Conference.

of his societies in America, using the ritual for the consecration of a bishop, but changing the title. He directed Dr. Coke to consecrate Francis Asbury to the same office as his associate in charge of the Wesleyan societies in America. A conference of the Methodist preachers in America was held in the week of Christmas, 1784, in Baltimore, and the Methodist Episcopal Church was organized. Asbury declined to receive the office of superintendent until to the appointment of John Wesley was added the vote of his fellow-preachers. Dr. Coke soon returned to England; by common consent the title "Bishop" soon took the place of the cumbrous word "Superintendent," and until 1800 Asbury was the sole incumbent of the office. To his tireless labors, wise plans, and strong leadership, the Methodist churches of America owe more than to any other one man.

5. Branches. The Methodist Episcopal Church was the parent body in this country, but from various differences in race, language, political rivalries, especially, in 1844, the agitation over the slavery question, many divisions took place. In April, 1939, the Uniting Conference forming The Methodist Church was held by representatives of The Methodist Episcopal Church; the Methodist Episcopal Church, South, and the Methodist Protestant Church, with a total membership in the United States of about eleven million.

4. The Christmas Conference.

6. Members.

7. Doctrines. These Methodist churches hold to the same theology, being strongly Arminian or free-will as opposed to the Calvinistic doctrine of predestination, and laying emphasis on the personal consciousness of salvation by every believer. They are also alike in their polity or organization; the local churches being grouped into districts under the charge of a presiding elder, although in the Methodist Episcopal Church his title was in 1908 changed to district superintendent; the districts united in annual conferences, and over all bishops who are appointed for life, though subject to retirement (in the Methodist Church) by the General Conference, the supreme law-making body, meeting every four years. Each pastor is appointed annually by the bishop in charge of his conference. In some branches of the church he can be reappointed as many times as may be desirable; in others his pastorate is limited to four years.

8. Organization.

The Church of the Brethren in Christ, now called the Evangelical United Brethren Church, was the first church in America not transplanted from the Old World. It arose in Pennsylvania and Maryland, under the earnest revival preaching of two men, Philip William Otterbein, born in Dillenburg, Germany, originally a minister of the German Reformed Church, and Martin Boehm, a Mennonite. Both preached in the German language, and formed German-speaking churches under the supervision of "unsectarian" ministers. In 1767, these two leaders met for the first time at a "great meeting" in a barn, near Lancaster, Pennsylvania, at which time the small Mr. Boehm preached with marked spiritual power. At the close of the sermon, the large Mr. Otterbein embraced the preacher and exclaimed, "We are brethren." From that greeting came the

X. United Brethren.

1. Origin.

2. Doctrines.

corporate name of the church, the words "in Christ" being added at the formal institution of the church in Frederick County, Maryland, in 1800. At that time, Otterbein and Boehm were elected bishops, and a government was adopted fashioned after the American democracy. While bishops are chosen, the church always has had but one order of preachers, and no episcopacy. All power is vested in the laity; all officers, including bishops, being elected for a term of four years by an equal number of ministers and laymen, conference superintendents always having been elected, not appointed. While

3. Polity. its polity and government differ from those of the Methodist Church, except that it has quarterly, annual, and general conferences, it preaches the same Arminian theology.

Services at first were exclusively in German, but now almost wholly in English. Church headquarters and printing establishment are at Dayton, Ohio. Its chief benevolent institution, the Otterbein Home, the largest in the United States, is located near Lebanon, Ohio. The members are conservative as

4. Division. to attire, oaths or affirmations and resistance to force.

After several years of discussion, a division occurred in 1889, a majority favoring a revision of the constitution of the church so as to remove the membership ban against those belonging to secret orders. The "Radicals" formed a new church, the "Liberals" being awarded all church property except in Michigan and Oregon.

5. Members. In Johnstown, Pennsylvania, November 16, 1946, there was a union between the Evangelical Church and the Church of the United Brethren in Christ. The combined membership totals slightly over seven hundred thousand.

The church bearing two names, both official, of "Disciples of Christ," and also "The Christian Church," unlike the other bodies already named in this chapter, was distinctly American in its origin. It began its history in 1804, after a great religious awakening in Tennessee and Kentucky, where the Rev. Barton W. Stone, a Presbyterian minister, withdrew from that denomination and organized a church at Cane Ridge, Bourbon County, Kentucky, of which the Bible, without any doctrinal statements was to be the only standard of faith, and the only name Christian.   A few years afterward the Rev. Alexander Campbell, a Presbyterian minister from Ireland, adopted the principle of baptism by immersion, and formed a Baptist church, but soon withdrew, and called his followers "Disciples of Christ."   Both Stone and Campbell established many churches, and in 1827 their congregations were united, forming one church in which both names, "Disciples" and "Christian," were recognized. The effort of both these men had been to unite all the followers of Christ in one body, with no creedal statement other than faith in Christ, and with no more definite name than "Disciples" or "Christians."

They accept both the Old and New Testament, but only the latter as the standard for Christians, with no specific statement of doctrine.   They practice baptism by immersion of believers only, not including infants, with the view that in the act of

XI. Disciples of Christ.

1. Origin.

2. Aims.

3. Doctrinal Standards.

4. Ecclesiastical System.

baptism "comes a divine assurance of remission of sins and acceptance with God." They are Congregational in their system, each church being independent of outside control, but uniting with the denomination for mission work at home and abroad. Their officers are elders chosen by the churches, pastors, deacons and evangelists, although they recognize no distinction between ministers and laymen. Throughout their history the Disciples of Christ have been zealous and aggressive in evangelism. They have a membership of slightly over one and a half million.

5. Growth.

Another similar body, also called "Christians," or "Christian Church," merged with the Congregationalists in 1931.

XII.
Unitarians.

The Unitarian churches in England and America are the modern representatives of the ancient Arians of the fourth and fifth centuries. They empha-

1. Doctrines.

size the human nature of Jesus Christ, and have thereby served the cause of Christian truth. But they deny to Jesus Christ Godhead or Diety, and they regard the Holy Spirit not as a Person but as an influence. They assert the being and unity of God, but not the Trinity or "three Persons in one God." They are generally opposed to the Calvinistic doctrine of predestination, believing with the Methodists in the freedom of the human will. They regard the Bible not as an authority in faith and conduct but as a valuable collection of literature.

2. Origin.

In America they appeared at first not as a sect but as a school of thought in the New England churches. In 1785, King's Chapel in Boston, then Protestant

Episcopal, adopted a creed and a liturgy omitting all recognition of the Trinity, and chose a minister of Unitarian opinions, the first church in New England of that faith. In 1805 a Unitarian, Henry Ware, was made professor of divinity in Harvard University; and in 1819 a Unitarian School of Theology was established in the same university, which since that time has been under Unitarian control. The name "Unitarian" as applied to the movement first appeared in 1815; and soon after this many of the oldest Congregational churches in New England became Unitarian; including the one founded by the Pilgrim Fathers in Plymouth. In the controversy that arose, more than one hundred and twenty- of the Congregational churches went over to the Unitarian views, without changing their names. The Unitarian body has embraced many leaders of thought in the United States, particularly in New England. Nearly all the Cambridge and Boston poets—Lowell, Longfellow, Holmes and Bryant, among them—were Unitarians. Yet the Unitarian churches have not won members in proportion to the Trinitarian or orthodox branch of Congregationalism. Their membership has shown a slight increase 3. Membership. in the past decade or more and now numbers about 75,000. In polity they are congregational, each local church being self-governing. They have no standard creed or confession of faith, and as a result, their ministers have the widest liberty and variety of opinion, some of them hardly to be distinguished from the "orthodox," others on the extreme of free-thought. But while uncertain in their doctrines, Unitarians have always been active in reform and all efforts of social service.

XIII.
Christian
Scientists.
1. Its
Founder.

The Church of Christ, Scientist, is composed of those who accept as authority the teachings of Mrs. Mary Baker Glover Eddy. She began to announce her principles in 1867, established an association of Christian Scientists in 1876, and organized her followers as a church in Boston, in 1879, with herself

2. Organization.

as pastor. Its members were twenty-six in number, but have increased to thousands, worshiping in a magnificent building, and known as "The Mother Church," exercising a certain control over all the churches and societies of the denomination. Mrs. Eddy died in 1910, and left no successor, but her teachings are embodied in a volume called "Science and Health." The various churches of Christian Science have no pastors, but instead in each church a "First Reader" taking charge of the services, and changed from time to time. Their

3. Belief.

doctrines are disseminated by lecturers, appointed by the parent church. Practically it is a system of healing disease of mind and body which teaches that all cause and effect is mental, and that sin, sickness, and death will be destroyed by a full understanding of the divine Principle of Jesus' teaching and healing.

4. Membership.

The membership figures are not available. The manual of the church forbids "the numbering of people and the reporting of such statistics for publication." Churches and societies number 3,049.

CHAPTER XXV.

THE CHURCHES IN CANADA.

ROMAN CATHOLIC. THE CHURCH OF ENGLAND.
METHODIST AND PRESBYTERIAN. UNITED
CHURCH AND OTHER DENOMINATIONS.

During the seventeenth century, while their fellow priests, with varying degrees of success and failure, of Christian work and secular negotiation, were extending the power of the Church of Rome in India and the Moluccas, in China and Japan, in Brazil and Paraguay, missionaries of the Society of Jesus were winning over to Catholicism the Huron Indians in what is now the Province of Ontario. As early as 1626, Jean de Brebeuf founded a mission on the forest-clad shores of Georgian Bay. Everywhere throughout a still wider region of forest and wilderness these and other pioneers of religion preached and suffered and struggled with the forces of nature, and of native barbarism, or died for the faith that was in them.

1. Seventeenth Century Pioneers of Religion.

With breviary and crucifix they wandered far. From the wave-beaten shores of Nova Scotia to the prairies of the unknown West, from the region of Hudson Bay to the mouth of the Mississippi, they passed in a succession of black-robed figures. They persevered in their mission "for the glory of God," for the advancement of the Order and of New France, until, as Bancroft, the historian, puts it, "Not a cape was turned, not a river was entered but a Jesuit led the way."

2. The
Roman
Catholic
Church.

As in the section of America which is now the United States, so in Canada the Roman Catholics were first to establish churches. French settlers brought with them the old religion as well as the old language, and cleave to both today. In Quebec, especially, the Catholic Church guided and modified and controlled the institutions of the province, the habits and customs of the French race, the morals and politics and loyalty of the people. A fairly recent religious census indicates that out of a total population of 11,500,000, there are almost five million Catholics, with nearly 2,900,000 in Quebec alone, and over 882,400 in Ontario.

3. The
Church of
England.

The Church of England, also called the Anglican Church, in all the English provinces was a dominant power in the early days, an influence for loyalty to the Crown, for education in the love of British institutions, for adherence to rule by a governing loyalist class, for devotion to the policy of early British governors. It held a high place in the government of all the provinces; took a vigorous position in matters of education, and did much, in coöperation with other denominations, to pioneer Western religious activities. The Anglican Church in Canada has a membership of 1,751,000, with 815,400 in Ontario, and 245,000 in British Columbia.

4. Metho-
dists and
Presby-
terians.

In the various divisions of the Christian Church in Canada the controversies of the Old Land were reproduced with more or less fidelity. The Church of England disputed over forms and ceremonies of High or Low Church practice just as they did in England. Methodism was divided into the Primitive Methodist Church, the Bible Christian Church and the Wesleyan Methodist Church, while its American affiliations and Canadian position brought into existence the new Methodist Episcopal Church and the Methodist New Connexion. Presbyterianism had its Church of Scotland in Canada, its Free Church Synod, its Presbyterian Church of the Lower Provinces, its United Presbyterian Church, its Canada Presbyterian Church. If, however, the denominations shared in the shaded differences of thought and creed which came to them from the Old Land, they also shared, immensely and beneficially, in the financial benefactions of the British churches and of the great missionary societies; while the Church of England in Canada received large sums from the British Parliament. The various Methodist churches were largely aided by funds from London, and their early missionaries were almost entirely supported from that source. So with the Presbyterian denominations and the well-known Glasgow Colonial Society and its practical work between 1825 and 1840.

In 1925 the Methodists united with the Congregationalists and part of the Presbyterians to form the United Church of Canada, with a population ᶜonstituency of over two millions, over one million being in the Province of Ontario alone. Many Presbyterian churches declined to join the union, and the Presbyterian Church in Canada carries on with over two hundred fifty thousand members.

5. United Church of Canada.

The Baptists, Lutherans, and other Protestant churches have always exercised a strong influence

6. Baptist and Lutheran.

in public affairs. The one public question in which the strong Baptist denomination of the Maritime Provinces was concerned was that of secular education. The Baptist population is about 480,000, with 193,000 in Ontario and 160,000 in the two provinces of New Brunswick and Nova Scotia. Lutherans number about 401,000, the greatest number being in Saskatchewan (115,000), with Ontario coming next (104,000).

7. Doukhobors and Mennonites. The interesting but troublesome sect known as the Doukhobors, who came from Russia at the beginning of the twentieth century, are for the most part settled in Saskatchewan and British Columbia, with a few in Alberta and Manitoba. They number about 16,000; peaceful, non-progressive people, caring little for education, and refusing to fight.

According to the 1951 census, there were 125,938 Mennonites in Canada.

8. Other Denominations. Other Christian bodies in Canada are the Adventists (18,000); Brethren and United Brethren (15,000); Christian (11,500); Church of Christ and Disciples of Christ (20,000); Christian Science (20,000); Evangelical Association (37,000); etc.

APPENDIX

CHAPTER I.

BLACKBOARD OUTLINE

Six. Gen. Per. Ch. Hist.

    I. **Per. Ap. Ch.** Asc. Chr. 30—Dea. St. J. 100.

    II. **Per. Per. Ch.** Dea. St. J. 100—Ed. Const. 313.

    III. **Per. Imp. Ch.** Ed. Const. 313—Fa. Wes. Ro. Emp. 476.

    IV. **Per. Med. Ch.** Fa. Wes. Ro. Emp. 476—Fa. Const. 1453.

    V. **Per. Ref. Ch.** Fa. Const. 1453—E. 30 Ye. W. 1648.

    VI. **Per. Mod. Ch.** E. 30 Ye W. 1648—20 Cent.

REVIEW QUESTIONS.

Into how many periods is church history divided? What is the name given to each period? With what event, and in what year does the first period begin and end? In what aspects is Christianity shown in the first period? Name the events and dates of the beginning and end of the second period. What are the great facts presented in the second period? What are the events and dates which bound the third period? Name some of the most important facts in the third period. Name and give the limits of the fourth period. What great facts are to be noticed in the fourth period? Give the events and dates which limit the fifth period. What are the greatest facts to be noted in the fifth period? Between what events and dates is the sixth period? Name some great movements which have appeared in the sixth period.

CHAPTER II.

BLACKBOARD OUTLINE

1. **Def.** Chr. Ch. is —.
2. **Beg.** D. Pen. 30 A. D.
3. **Endow.** (1) Illu. (2) Emp. (3) Abi. pres.
4. **Loc.** Jer.
5. **Mem.** J. (1) Heb. (2) Hellen. (3) Pros.
6. **Lead.** Pet. Jhn.
7. **Gov.**
8. **Doct.** (1) Mes. J. (2) Res. J. (3) Ret. J.
9. **Gosp.** Test.
10. **Mir.** (1) Heal. (2) Judge. (3) Div. Pow.
    (4) Steph.
11. **Spir. Bro.** "Comm." (1) Vol. (2) Sma.
    Com. (3) Selec. (4) Expec. (5) Fail.
    (6) Evils.
12. **One Def.** Lac. Miss. Zea.

REVIEW QUESTIONS.

What are the events and dates bounding the First General Period? What is the name given to the church during the first part of this period? Give a definition of the Christian Church. When did the church begin its history? Up to what time were the disciples forbidden to preach Christ as the Messiah-King? What endowment came upon the followers of Christ, and when did it come? What were the effects of this endowment? Where was the church located in its earliest years? Of what race or people were all its members? Name three classes of people in the membership of the church. Who were the leaders of the church in the first days? How was the church governed? What were its three leading doctrines? Who were its preachers? What miracles are narrated? What were the effects of these miracles? How was the spirit of brotherhood shown? What is said about communism in the early church? What was the one fault or defect in the pentecostal church?

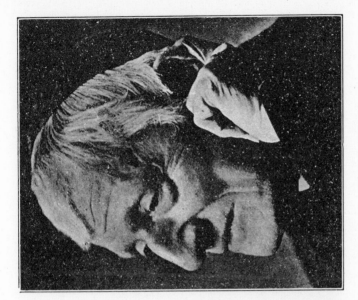

CARDINAL NEWMAN

JOHN WESLEY

CHAPTER III.

BLACKBOARD OUTLINE.

Ap. Ch. Part 2.   The Exp. Ch. 35–50 A. D.
　　　　Imp. Per.   Stages in Exp. Move.

1. **Ste. Pre.**
2. **Sau. Pers.**
3. **Phil. in Sam.**
4. **Pet. at Jop. and Caes.** (Vis. Corn.)
5. **Sau. Conv.**
6. **Ch. at Ant.** Founders. Members. Bar. Sau. "Chr. Aid."
7. **Fir. Miss. Jour.** (1) Two Workers. (2) John Mark. (3) Cities. S. P. A. I. L. D. (4) Preac. Syn. (5) Re-visit. and organized.
8. **Counc. Jer.** "Conserv. *vs.* Progress." Dissension. Meeting. Decision.

SUGGESTIONS FOR STUDY.

Read carefully Acts 6 to 15, inclusive; and look up all the text-references in the chapter.

Memorize the eight points in the subdivision.

Locate every place named upon a map. On the map of Palestine note the places in the journeys of Philip; of Peter to Joppa and Cæsarea; of Saul from Jerusalem to Damascus and Arabia.

On a map including Palestine, Syria, and Asia Minor, follow the journeys of Saul from Damascus to Jerusalem, to Tarsus, to Antioch. On the same map trace the route of the First Missionary Journey; and the journey of Paul and Barnabas from Antioch to the Council at Jerusalem and returning.

REVIEW QUESTIONS.

Why is this an important subdivision in church history? Name its eight principal stages. Who began the movement for the gospel to the Gentile world? What was the result of this man's preaching upon himself and upon the church? How did Saul while still an enemy help the advance of the gospel? Who was Philip? What part did Philip take in the enlarging movement? Who were the Samaritans? What vision did Peter have? What followed Peter's vision? Give an account of the conversion of Saul. Name the places to which Saul journeyed after his conversion. Where was a church established of Jews and Gentiles mingled? How did this church arise? How was the news of this church received at Jerusalem? Who was sent to examine it? How did this messenger feel, and what did he do? Whom did he associate with himself in the work of this church? What name was given in that city to the followers of Christ? Who were the missionaries first sent out by the church? What were the methods that they pursued? What places in their order did they visit? For what purpose was a council held in Jerusalem? Who took part in it? What were the conclusions of the council?

CHAPTER IV.

BLACKBOARD OUTLINE.

III. Ch. Am. Gent. C. J. 50 – Mart. St. P. 68.

1. **Auth.** Ac. Ep. P. 1 Pet. Trad
2. **Field.** Rom. Emp. Oth. La.
3. **Mem.** Inc. Gent. Dec. Jew.
4. **Lead.** Pau. Pet. Jam.
5. **St. Pau. Jour.** (1) Fir. Jour. As. Min.
   (2) Sec. Jour. Rev. As. Min. Tro. Ph. Thess. Ber. Ath. Cor. Eph. Jer. Ant.
   (3) Thir. Jour. Syr. Cil. Eph. Mac. Tro. Mil. (Eld. Eph.) Jer. Arrest.
   (4) Four. Jour. (Pris.). Comp. Lu. Aris. Voyage. Rome. Epistles. Liberty.
6. **Fir. Imp. Per.** Nero. Mart. Pet. 67. Mart. Pau. 68.
7. **Lit. of Per.** Mat. Mk. Luke. Ep. Pau. Jas. 1 Pet. 2 Pet.(?).

For Paul's Second Journey read Acts 15:36 to 18:22.   For his
Third Journey, read Acts 18:23 to 21:35.   For his imprisonment and
Fourth Journey, read Acts 22 to 28.   Some of the questions are
answered in the reading, not in the text-book.

REVIEW QUESTIONS.

What is the third subdivision of the Period of the Apostolic
Church?   With what dates and events did it begin and end?   What
was the field of the church at this time?   Of what races was the
church now composed?   Who were the three leaders during the
period?   Review Paul's First Journey.   From what place did Paul
start on his Second Missionary Journey?   Who was his companion?
Who joined him later?   What places of his First Journey did he
revisit?   What new places did he visit in Asia?   What new places
in Europe?   Can you tell his experiences in any of those places?
What letters were written on this journey?   Where did his journey
end?   What was the result of his Second Journey?   What places
did Paul visit on his Third Journey?   Where was he for the longest
time?   State his route on his return from the Third Journey.   Where
did Paul's Third Journey end?   What epistles were written during
this journey?   In what circumstances was Paul for some time after
this?   What was Paul's condition during his Fourth Journey?
What places did he visit?   What took place at Rome?   What letters did he write while a prisoner?   What can be told of Paul's
later years?   What emperor began the first imperial persecution
of the Christians?   What caused this persecution?   Who suffered
martyrdom at that time?   What was the Christian literature of
the period?

CHAPTER V.

BLACKBOARD OUTLINE.

Ag. Shad. Mart. St. P. 68—Dea. St. J. 100.

Gloom of Pers. Little known.

1. **Fa. Jer.** 70. Rebellion. Vesp. Tit. Christians.
   Results.
2. **Sec. Imp. Per.** 90–95. Dom. St. John.
3. **Comp. N. T.** Recog. later.
4. **Cond. Ch.** (1) Ext. Num. (2) Doct. Sys.
   (3) Inst. (a) Bap. (b) Lor. D. (c) Lor. Sup. (d)
   East. Sun. (4) Off. Apos. Bish. Eld. Dea. (5)
   Worsh. (6) Spir. Stat.

REVIEW QUESTIONS.

Name the four subdivisions in the history of the Apostolic Church. Why is the last subdivision called "the age of shadows"? Between what dates was this subdivision? What was the first important event named? Give account of this event. What was its effect upon the Christian church? What emperor led in the second imperial persecution of the Christians? What was the date of this persecution? What happened to one of the apostles during his persecution? What books of the New Testament were the last in being written? What is said of the numbers and extent of the church at the close of this period? What classes of people did the church represent? What was its doctrinal system? What were the institutions of the church? How was baptism observed? How was the Lord's Supper observed? What officers of the church are named? What was the plan of service in the meetings of the church? What was the spiritual state of the church at the end of the first century?

CHAPTER VI.

BLACKBOARD OUTLINE.

Per. Ch. (De. St. J. 100—Ed. Const. 313).
I. Caus. Imp. Per. 1. Hea. hosp. Chr. exc.
    2. Id. Wor. int. w. li. 3. Wor. emp. 4. Jud.
    rec. 5. Sec. Meet. Chr. 6. Chr. equal.
    7. Bus. int.
II. Stag. Per. 1. Traj. Ant. Pius. 96–161. Sim.
    Ign. 2. Mar. Aurel. 161–180 Poly. Just.
    Mar. 3. Sept. Sev. 193–211. Per. Fel.
    4. Dec. 249–251. 5. Val. 258. Cyp. Sex.
    6. Dioc. 303–310. Edict. Cons. 313.

REVIEW QUESTIONS.

Name the second general period of church history. With what
events and dates did it begin and end? What is the most prominent fact in the history of this period? In what centuries was the
church persecuted by the Roman emperors? What kind of Roman
emperors were the most severe in their persecution? Name seven
causes which account for these imperial persecutions. What was
the attitude of heathenism toward new objects of worship? What
was the spirit of Christianity toward other forms of worship? How
was the Jewish religion regarded by the government? How did this
affect the Christian religion, at first and later? How were the
secret meetings of Christians regarded? What was the effect of
the equalizing tendencies of the Christian Church? How did some
business interests promote persecution of the church? Was the
persecution of the Christians continuous during those centuries?
What was the condition of the church most of the time during those
centuries? What emperors persecuted the church before 100 A. D.?
Who were known as "the five good emperors"? How were the
Christians treated under their rule? What leading Christians suffered martyrdom at that time? What especially great and good
emperor became a persecutor of the church? What were his

motives? Who were martyrs during his reign? Who is named as the third persecuting emperor of this period? Who suffered under this emperor? What good edict was issued by Caracalla, and how did it benefit the Christians? Who was the fourth persecuting emperor? What relief followed the death of this emperor? Who was the sixth persecuting emperor? Who perished in his reign? Give an account of the sixth and last of the persecuting emperors? What works of this emperor afterward became tokens of the triumph of Christianity?

CHAPTER VII.

BLACKBOARD OUTLINE.

THE PER. CHUR. PART II.

III.   **Form. N. T. Canon.**   Writ. 110.   Canon Lat. Doubtful Bks. Councils. 300 A. D. "N. T. Apoc."

IV.   **Gro. Eccl. Org.**   Apost.   "Bish. Eld."   125 Bish.   Causes.   1. Loss. ap. auth.   2. Gro. and ext. Chu.   3. Persec.   4. Sects. and Hercs.   5. Anal. Imp. gov.

V.   **Devel. Doct.**   Emphasis on bel.   Ap. cr. Schoo. theol.   1. Alexan. 180 (Pant. Clem. Orig.).   2. As. Min. (Iren.).   3. No. Afr. Carth. (Tertul. Cyp.).

REVIEW QUESTIONS.

Name the two subjects already considered in this period. What is the third subject? What is the difference between the books and the canon? What books in our New Testament were for a time disputed? What books not now in the Bible were accepted in some of the churches? How were the books finally agreed upon?

What is said about the ecclesiastical organization of the early church? What two orders were originally the same? When do we find the organization complete? What was the form of government established in the church? Name five causes for the establishment of this form. How did the system of government in the empire lead to the system in the church?

What were the teachings emphasized in the apostolic period? What change came later in the church? What creedal statement was the earliest formed? Where did schools of theology arise? Name some of the leading teachers and expositors in each school.

CHAPTER VIII.

BLACKBOARD OUTLINE.

```
  VI.  Ris. Sec. Her.  1. Gnos.  2. Ebion.  3. Mani.
       4. Mont.
 VII.  Cond. Ch.  1. Pur. Ch.  2. Uni. Tea.  3. Org.
       Ch.  4. Grow. Ch.
```

REVIEW QUESTIONS.

What promoted the rise of sects and heresies in the church? Name four of the leading sects. State the teachings of each of these sects. Why is it difficult to know precisely what these sects taught?

What were four aspects in the condition of the church at the close of the persecutions? What will give some clue as to its numbers?

CHAPTER IX.

BLACKBOARD OUTLINE.

I. Vic. Chr. 305–324 A. D.

1. **Cons. Fir. Chr. Emp.**   Max. Cons. Milv. Br. 312. Vision Victory. Edic. Tol. 313. Sol. emp. 323. Char. Const.
2. **Good Res. Ch.**   (1) Per. ceas.   (2) Chu. res. "Basil."   (3) Sac. ceas.   (4) Tem. Consec. (5) Endow. Chur.   (6) Priv. cler.   (7) Sun. obs.
3. **Good Res. State.**   (1) Cruc. abol.   (2) Inf. dis.   (3) Slav. mod.   (4) Glad. gam. supp.
4. **Evil. Res.**   (1) Every. in ch.   (2) Pag. u$_s$. (3) Worl. ch.   (4) Un. ch. stat. East. West.

REVIEW QUESTIONS.

What is the title of the Third General Period? With what events and what dates did it begin and end?

What was the most prominent event of this period? What contrast is given between two dates not far apart in the history of the church and the empire?

By what emperor was Christianity recognized? With whom did he contest for the imperial power? What was his vision as reported? What edict did he issue and when? What followed his becoming sole emperor? What was his personal character?

Name seven good results that followed the recognition of Christianity in the empire. Give a statement of what was involved in each of those seven results.

Name some good results to the state from the victory of Christianity. What form of execution ceased and why? What was the effect of Christianity upon the lives of infants? How was the treatment of slaves affected? What took place with regard to the gladiatorial games?

What results for evil were also brought about by the victory of Christianity? What was the evil effect on the church? What pagan usages arose in the churches? Wherein was the spiritual

tone of the church influenced?   What harm came from the union
of the church with the state?

CHAPTER X.

BLACKBOARD OUTLINE.

Per. III.   Imp. Ch.   Part II.

II. **Foun. Const. 325.   1. Nee.   2. Loc.   3. Cap.
and Ch.   4. St. Soph.**

III. **Div. Emp.   Bound.   Dang.   Diocl.   Const.
E. and W.   G. and L.**

IV. **Supp. Heath.   1. Const. Tol.   2. Succ. Int.
(1) Endow.   (2) Rites.   (3) Temp. Dem.
(4) Anti-Chr. Bks.**

V. **Cont. and Coun.   1. Doc. Trin. Ari. *vs.* Ath.
Coun. Nic. 325.   2. Nat. Chr. Apoll. Coun.
Const. 381.   3. Sin. and Salv. Pelag. Doc.
Augus. Coun. Carth. 418.**

VI. **Ris. Monas.   1. Orig.   2. Foun. Anth.   3. Pill.
Sai.   4. Mon. in Eur. Bene. Rul.**

REVIEW QUESTIONS.

Name the five subjects in this chapter.   Why was a new capital
needed for the empire?   Where was the capital founded?   Why
was that a wise choice of location?   What were the relations between
the emperor and the head of the church in the capital?   Give an
account of a celebrated church building in that city.

Why was the empire divided?   Who began the division?   Who
completed it?   Where was the line drawn between the two sections
of the empire?   What languages were spoken in the two sections?

How was heathenism treated by the successors of Constantine?
What was Constantine's attitude toward the heathen religions?
What edicts were after his time issued against the old religions?
What was the effect of these laws?

When did great controversies arise in the church?   Over what
subjects were the controversies?   Who was Arius?   What was his

teaching? Who opposed Arius? What was the view of this opponent of Arius? What council considered the question? How was the question settled? What was the result later? What was the heresy of Apollinaris? What council undertook to decide the question? Over what was the Pelagian controversy? Who was Pelagius? What were the views against Pelagius? What council undertook the decision of that question?

What was the origin of monasticism? Who was its founder? What were the pillar saints? What was the tendency of the monastic life in Europe? Who regulated it?

CHAPTER XI.

BLACKBOARD OUTLINE.

PER III. THE IMP. CHU.

I. Vic. Chris.
II. Foun. Cons.
III. Div. Emp.
IV. Sup. Heath.
V. Cont. and Coun.
VI. Ris. Mon.
VII. Gro. Pow. Ro. Ch. 1. Caus. 1. Anal. Imp. Ru. 2. Ass. Apos. Auth. 3. Char. Ro. Ch. (1) Able bish. (2) Ortho. Ch. (3) Prac. Chr. 4. Trans. Cap.
VIII. Down. Wes. Rom. Emp. 1. Caus. (1) Rich. Emp. Cov. (2) Rom. Unu. War. (3) Emp. Weak. Civ. War. (4) Mov. As. Tri. 2. Barb. Invas. (1) Visig. (2) Vand. (3) Burg. (4) Fran. (5) Sax. Ang. (6) Huns. (451 Chal.) (7) Fa. Ro. 476. 3. Chu. and Conv. Barb.
IX. Leaders. 1. Ath. 293–373. 2. Amb. Mil. 340–397. 3. John Chr. 345–407. 4. Jer. 340–420. 5. Aug. 354–430.

REVIEW QUESTIONS.

Name the first six subdivisions of the Period of the Imperial Church? What is the seventh subject? What caused and aided the power of the Roman Church and its bishops? What apostolic authority was invoked for its claims? How did the character of the church and its bishops aid this progress of power? What was the effect of the transfer of the capital?

What was the seeming condition of the empire under Constantine? What was its real condition? Give the statement of four causes of the barbarian inroads. Name the seven barbarian conquests, from whence each came, and the part of the empire affected? When did the Western Roman Empire end, and by whom was it ended? How did these invasions affect the church and its relations?

Name five of the great leaders of the church during this period. Give a statement of the life and influence of each leader.

CHAPTER XII.

BLACKBOARD OUTLINE.

IV. Gen. Per. F. W. R. Emp. 476—Fa. Const. 1453.

I. **Dev. Pap. Pow.** ch. and sta.
1. **Sta. Gro.** 590–1073. Greg. I–Greg. VII.
    (1) "Angli-angeli." Miss. Const. Doc.
2. **Causes of Power.** (1) Pow. Right. (2) Rival. Sec. Rul. (3) Cons. Emp. Ch. (4) "Pi. Frau."
    (a) Don. Const. (b) Dec. Isa. Evidences. (1) Lang. (2) Tit. (3) Quot. (4) Lett.
3. **Sta. Culm.** (1) Hild. Greg. VII. (a) Ref. Cler. (b) Fre. Ch. (c) Ch. Supr. (2) Inno. III. Statements. (a) Otho. (b) Rome. (c) Phil. Aug. (d) John.
4. **Sta. of Dec.** (1) Bonif. (2) Bab. Cap. (3) Coun. Cons.

REVIEW QUESTIONS.

What is the most prominent fact in the history of the church during the Middle Ages? Wherein was the difference between the claims of the pope in earlier ages and during the Middle Ages? What were the three stages of this development?

Between what years was the first stage of papal power? Between what ruling popes was it? Who was the pope called "the Great"? What were some things accomplished by him? Name four reasons or causes for the growth of papal power. What were some "pious frauds" perpetrated during those ages? Define and explain each of those frauds. What evidences afterward proved their falsity?

Under what pope was the culmination of papal claims reached? State some of that pope's achievements. Over what rulers, and in what events, was he victorious? What is meant by "to go to Canossa?" What other pope, and when, was supreme? What were some of his claims? Over what rulers did he exercise power?

What led to the decline of papal power? What pope showed by his experiences the change of affairs? What is meant by the Babylonish Captivity, and when was it? How was this period of captivity ended?

CHAPTER XIII.

BLACKBOARD OUTLINE.

II. **The Ris. of Moham.** 200 mill.

1. **Found.** Moh. 570. Heg. 622. Conq. D. 632.
2. **His Rel.** Isl. (1) God. (2) Foreor. (3) Ang. (4) Kor. (5) Prop. (6) Hereaf.
3. **Prog.** (1) Pal. Syr. (2) Gr. Emp. (3) Pers. Ind. (4) Afr. Sp. Tours. 732.
4. **Elem. Pow.** (1) Fai. (2) Gre. Sub. (3) Isl. rel.
5. **Fav. Asp. Moh.** (1) Simp. doc. (2) Opp. im. wor. (3) Rej. pr. sai. med. (4) Abs. Liq. (5) Lit. Sci.
6. **Unfav. Asp.** (1) Conv. by Conq. (2) Sec. rel. (3) View of G. (4) View of Chr. (5) Conc. heav. (6) Deg. Wom. (7) Lac. adm. abil.

REVIEW QUESTIONS.

What great religion arose in the early Middle Ages? What is now the number of its followers? Who was its founder? What can you tell of his life? What is meant by "the Hegira"?

Name the six great doctrines of the Mohammedan faith. Give an account of its early successes. What were the alternatives given to the nations by the conquerors? Name the lands in the East overrun by the Mohammedans. What lands in the West were conquered by them? At what place and time, and by what leader was their progress stopped?

What were the elements of power that gave the Mohammedan religion its success? What was the condition of the eastern world? Name some good elements in the Mohammedan religion. What is its attitude toward strong drink? Wherein has the Mohammedan religion failed?

CHAPTER XIV.

BLACKBOARD OUTLINE.

III. **The Ho. Rom. Emp.** Cent. IX–XIX.

1. **Found.** Char. (Karl.) 742–814. **Kg-Fra.** Emp. 800 A. D.
2. **Emp.** Weak. desc. Dev. states. Lim. Emp.
3. **Emper.** 1. Hen. I. (Fow.) 919–936. 2. Otho. I. (Gre.) 936–973. 3. Fred. Barb. (1152–1190). 4. Fred. II. "Enigma." 5. Rud. Haps. 1273– 1291. 6. Char. V. (1519–1556). Abdic.
4. **Emp. and Pop.** Riv. War. Greg. VII–Innoc. III.
5. **Dec. and Fall.** Voltaire. 1806. Fran. II.

IV. **Sep. Lat. Gr. Ch.** 1. Doc. 2. Usage. 3. Pol. Cau. 4. Clai. Ro.

REVIEW QUESTIONS.

What governmental system arose in the Middle Ages? What was the condition of Europe before it appeared? How long did it last?

Who was its founder? When did he live? What is said of his ancestry and career? How was he made emperor? What was his character as a ruler?

What caused a limitation in the imperial authority? Name six of the most important emperors. State some facts about each of those emperors. What were the relations between the emperors and the popes? What led to the decline in the imperial power? What was said of the empire by a witty Frenchman? When did the empire come to an end? Who was the last of these emperors? How was the division between the two great branches of the church effected? What was the doctrinal cause of the separation? What four customs in the usages of the East and West were different? How did the claim of one church lead to separation?

CHAPTER XV.

BLACKBOARD OUTLINE.

Med. Ch. Part. IV.
V. **The Crus.** 1095–1270.

1. **Orig.**
2. **The Sev. Crus.**
   (1) Fir. Cru. 1095–1099. Pet. Her. God-Boul.
       Km. Jer. 1099–1187.
   (2) Sec. Cru. 1147–1149. Lou. VII. Conr. III.
   (3) Thir. Cru. 1189–1191. Fred. Phil. Rich.
   (4) Fou. Cru. 1201–1204. Const. tak.
   (5) Fif. Cru. 1228, 1229. Fred. II.
   (6) Six. Cru. 1248–1254. Lou. IX.
   (7) Sev. Cru. 1270–1272. Lou. IX. Prin.
       Edw.
3. **Cau. Fail.**
   (1) Diss. Lead.
   (2) Lim. View.
4. **Good Res.**
   (1) Pil. pro.
   (2) Mos. Agg. Ch.
   (3) Nat. Acq.
   (4) Imp. Tra.
   (5) Pow. Ch.

REVIEW QUESTIONS.

What great series of religious wars took place during the Middle Ages? What was the cause of these wars? How many crusades are named? Tell the story, name the leaders, and give the results of the First Crusade. Give the date, leaders, and results of the Second Crusade. Who were prominent in the Third Crusade, and what was its result? Give an account of the Fourth Crusade. The Fifth Crusade. The Sixth Crusade. The Seventh Crusade. Why did the Crusades fail? What good results came from them?

CHAPTER XVI.

BLACKBOARD OUTLINE.

VI.　**Devel. Monas.**　1. **Ord.** (1) **Ben.** (2) **Cis.**
　　　(3) **Fran.** (4) **Dom.**
　　　2. **Ben. Mon.** (1) **Cen. pea.** (2) **Hosp.**
　　　(3) **Ref.** (4) **Pro. agri.** (5) **Lib.** (6) **Edu.**
　　　(7) **Miss.**
　　　3. **Evil Res.** (1) **Cel. Lif.** (2) **Seclu.** (3)
　　　Wealth. (4) **Rapacity.**
VII.　**Med. Dev. Art and Lit.** 1. **Univ.** 2. **Cath.**
　　　3. **Lit.** 4. **Art.**

REVIEW QUESTIONS.

State the five subjects already considered in the Period of the Medieval Church. Name the five subjects contained in this chapter. How did monasticism originate? What was the principal difference between the eastern and western monasticism? Name the four principal orders of monks in Europe. Give an account of the first order named. What was the origin of the second order? The third order? The fourth order? What were some benefits of the monastic system? What were some of its evils?

What were some of the developments during the Middle Ages in art and literature?

CHAPTER XVII.

BLACKBOARD OUTLINE.

VIII. **Beg. Rel. Ref.** 1. Albi. 1170. 2. Wald.
1170. 3. J. Wyc. 1324–1384. 4. J. Hu.
1369–1415 5. J. Savon. 1452–1498.
IX. **Fa. Const.** 1453.
X. **Sch. and Lead.** 1. Ans. 2. Abel. 3. Bern.
4. T. Aqui.

REVIEW QUESTIONS.

What five attempts at the reformation of the church were made during the later Middles Ages? Give an account of each one of these efforts. What great event is regarded as the conclusion of the Medieval period? Give an acount of this event. Name four great scholars and leaders of thought in the Middles Ages. Give an account of each leader.

CHAPTER XVIII.

BLACKBOARD OUTLINE.

PER. V. THE REF. CHU.
I. **Antec. Forc.** 1. Ren. 2. Inv. Prin. 3. Spi.
Nat.
II. **Ref. Germ.** Mar. Luth. 1. Indul. 2. Thes.
3. Bur. Pap. B. 4. Die. Wor. 5. Wart.
6. Prot. Na.

REVIEW QUESTIONS.

What is the subject of this chapter? Name and describe three antecedent forces leading to the Reformation. How did the Renaissance promote the Reformation? How did the invention of printing aid it? How did the growing spirit of nationality aid the Reformation? In what country did the Reformation begin? Who was its leader? Name the six stages mentioned in the progress of the Reformation in Germany. What were "the indulgences"? How did the sale of the indulgences become the immediate occasion of the Reformation? With what date and what event did the Reformation open? What was the papal bull? How did Luther treat it? When was the Diet of Worms held? What took place at that meeting? Where was Luther in seclusion? What did he do at that time? How did the name "Protestant" arise?

CHAPTER XIX.

BLACKBOARD OUTLINE.

III. **Ref. in Oth. Lan.**
    1. Switz. Zwing. 1517–1531 Calv.
    2. Scan. Kgdm. Den. Swe. Nor.
    3. Franc. Lef. Mass. St. Bar. 1572.
    4. Neth. Holl. Bel.
    5. Eng. (1) Hen. VIII. Mor. Tyn. Cran.
        (2) Edw. VI. (3) Qu. Mar. (4) Qu. Eliz.
    6. Scot. J. Kno.
IV. **Prin. Ref.** 1. Scr. Rel. 2. Rat. Rel. **3. Per.** Rel. 4. Spir. Rel. 5. Nat. Rel.

REVIEW QUESTIONS.

Who led the Reformation in Switzerland? Give an account of its origin. Who was its later leader, and what was his great work? What nations are included in Scandinavia? What was the history of the Reformation in those lands? Tell the story of the Reformation in France. By what event was its progress in France checked? What took place in the Netherlands? How did the reform begin in England? Who were among its leaders? What part did four successive sovereigns of England take? Give an account of the Reformation in Scotland. Who led and shaped the Reformation in Scotland?

CHAPTER XX.

BLACKBOARD OUTLINE.

V. **Coun. Ref.** 1. Ref. with Ch. (Coun. Tr.).
2. Or. Jes. (Loy.) 3. Act. Per. 4. Miss.
Eff. 5. Thir. Ye. War.
VI. **Lead. Per.** 1. Des. Eras. 2. Mar. Luth. 3.
Ph. Mel. 4. Th. Cran. 5. J. Kno. 6. Ign.
Loy. 7. St. Fr. Xav.

REVIEW QUESTIONS.

Name the five general principles of the reformed religion. Explain each of those principles. What is meant by "the Counter-Reformation"? How was reform within the church attempted? Give account of the great council. What order was established, and for what purpose? What was the history of that order? What active persecutions were undertaken? What missionary efforts were made by the Roman Church? What was the Thirty Years' War? When did it begin and end? What treaty of peace was finally made? Name seven leaders of the Reformation period. Who of these were Protestants? Who were Roman Catholics? Give an account of each leader.

CHAPTER XXI.

BLACKBOARD OUTLINE.

Per. VI. Mod. Ch. From E. Th. Ye. W. (1648)
to Cent. XX. (1900).

I. **Pur. Move.** Two par. Eliz. Char. I. Cromw.
Pres. Cong. Bap.

II. **Wes. Rev.** John W. Chas. W. Geo. White.
"Meth."

III. **Ratio. Move.** Seml. Strau. Schleir. Neau.
Tho.

IV. **Oxf. Move.** 1. Names. 2. Aim. 3. Beg.
4. Lead. 5. Tend. 6. Res.

REVIEW QUESTIONS.

What is the title of the Sixth Period in Church History? Name all the six periods. With what events and dates did the modern period begin and end? Name the five great movements in this period. Give an account of the Puritan movement under the successive rulers of England. What three denominations arose from it?

What was the condition of Christianity in England in the early part of the Eighteenth Century? What three leaders arose? What revival took place? Give account of this revival, its leader, and its results.

What is meant by the rationalistic movement? Where and when did it originate? Name some of its leaders. Who aided in leading the church from rationalism? What were some results of the rationalistic movement? What was the Oxford movement? What were some other names of it, and why were they given? How did the movement originate? Who were its leaders? What were its aims? What were some of its results.

CHAPTER XXII.

BLACKBOARD OUTLINE.

V. **Mod. Miss. Move.** 1. Miss. Ear. Ch. 2. Neg. Lat. 3. Morav. Miss. 4. Eng. Miss. (Car.) 5. Amer. Miss. (Hays. P. M.). Am. Bd. 6. Pres. Miss. Cond.

VI. **Lead. Mod. Per.** 1. R. Hook. (1553–1600). 2. T. Cart. (1535–1613). 3. Jon. Edw. (1703–1758). 4. J. Wes. (1703–1791). 5. J. H. New. (1801–1890).

VII. **Ch. Cent. XX.** 1. Doc. 2. Spir. 3. Serv.

REVIEW QUESTIONS.

How long was early Christianity a missionary institution? What was its condition during much of the medieval period? Who were the first missionaries after this Reformation? What church began Protestant missions? Who was the founder of modern English missions? Give an account of his life. What was "the haystack meeting"? What resulted from it? Name six leaders of the modern church. Give an account of each leader. What are the three traits prominent in the church at the opening of the twentieth century?

CHAPTER XXIII.

BLACKBOARD OUTLINE.

Chu. in U. S. 168–145.

I. **Rom. Cath.** 1. Span.   2. Fren.   3. Eng.
    4. Imm.   5. Gov.

II. **Prot. Epis.** (Ch. Eng.) 1. Va.   2. N. Y.
    3. Am. Rev.   4. Bish.   5. Mem.   6. Org.

III. **Cong.** 1. Pilg.   2. Org.   3. Gro.   4. Doc.
    5. Mem.

IV. **Ref. Chu.** 1. Ref. Ch. Am. (R. P. D. C.).
    2. Ref. Ch. U. S.   3. Doc.   4. Org.

V. **Bap.** 1. Prin.   2. Sys.   3. Spir.   4. Orig.
    5. In Am.   6. Bod.   7. Miss.

VI. **Fri. (Quak.).** 1. Fox.   2. Teach.   3. Mass.
    4. N. J.   5. Penn.   6. Div.   7. Mem.

REVIEW QUESTIONS.

What church was the earliest on American soil? For what reason? From what two countries did its numbers come? What was the religious condition and prospect of the continent about 1750? What colony was settled by this church? How has the church received its increase? How is it organized? How large is its membership.

What Protestant church was earliest in this continent? Give an account of its beginnings. What was its condition during and immediately after the Revolution? Who were its first bishops? How large is it at present? What is its form of organization?

How did the congregational churches originate? What is their system of organization? Give some account of their growth. What are their doctrines? What is their present membership?

Where did the Reformed Church arise. What was its name? In what colony was it established? What has been its history? What other Reformed Church is there? What was its origin? What are the doctrines of these churches? How are they organized?

How many denominations of Baptists are in the United States?
What are their numbers?   What are their distinctive principles?
How are they organized?   When and where did they arise in
Europe?   Who was their founder in the colonies?   What state did
they establish?   What part have they taken in foreign missions?

Who are the Friends?   By what other name are they known?
Who was their founder?   What were his teachings?   How were
the Quakers treated in the early colonies?   Where did they settle?
What state was founded by them, and under what circumstances?
What division took place among them?   What is their present
membership?

CHAPTER XXIV.

BLACKBOARD OUTLINE.

VII.   **Luth.**   1. N. Y.   2. Del. Riv.   3. Gro.
4. Mem.   5. Org.   6. Doc.

VIII.   **Pres.**   1. Ori.   2. Rev. War.   3. Div.
4. Mem.   5. Doc.   6. Gov.

IX.   **Meth.**   1. N. Y. and Md.   2. Asbury.
3. Fir. Conf.   4. Chr. Conf.   5. Bran.
6. Mem.   7. Doc.   8. Org.

X.   **Un. Breth.**   1. Ori.   2. Doc.   3. Pol.   4.
Div.   5. Mem.

XI.   **Dis. Chr. (Chr.).**   1. Orig.   2. Aims.   3.
Doc. Stan.   4. Ecc. Sys.   5. Gro.

XII.   **Unit.**   1. Doc.   2. Orig.   3. Mem.

XIII.   **Chr. Sci.**   1. Found.   2. Org.   3. Belief.
4. Mem.

REVIEW QUESTIONS.

How did the Lutheran churches originate?   Where did they first
appear in this country?   In what other places did they settle?   How
have they grown?   What is their membership?   How are they
organized?   What are their doctrinal beliefs.

From what three lands did the Presbyterians come to America? Give an account of them in Scotland and in England. Where were they first established in America? Who was their leader in organizing the church? What part did they take in the Revolutionary War? What divisions have arisen among them? How many branches do they embrace? What are their doctrines and organization?

What two places and leaders are named for the beginnings of Methodism in the United States? Who were the earliest missionaries to this country? Who was the greatest of their early leaders? When and how was the church organized? How many branches are there in this church? How large is it? What are its doctrines? What is its form of organization?

Who are the Brethren? How did they originate? What are their doctrines and polity? How were they united in 1946?

What church has two official names? How did these different names arise? Who were the founders of this church? What are their doctrinal standards? How are they organized? What has been their growth?

What ancient people do the Unitarians represent? What are the Unitarian doctrines? How did they arise in this country? What influence have they exerted? What are their numbers? In what efforts have they been prominent?

Who was the founder of the Christian Science Church? Where did it originate? What are its views? Why is its membership not available?

CHAPTER XXV.

BLACKBOARD OUTLINE.

   I. **Sev. Cen. Pioneers.** 1. Soc. Jes. 2. Jean de Brebeuf in Ont. 3. Nov. Sco. to West. 4. Hud. Bay to Miss.

  II. **Rom. Cath.** 1. Fr. set. in Can. 2. Cath. Ch. Que. 3. 1931 rel. cen.

 III. **Ch. Eng.** 1. Pow. in Ear. Days. 2. Loy. to Gov. 3. Mem. in Can. 4. Mem. in Ont. 5. Mem. B. C.

 IV. **Meth. and Pres.** 1. Prim. Meth. Ch. 2. Bib. Chris. Ch. 3. Wes. Meth. Ch. 4. Meth. Epis. Ch. 5. Meth. New Con. 6. Ch. of Scot. in Can. 7. Free Ch. 8. Pres. Ch. of Lower Prov. 8. U. P. Ch. 9. Can. Pres. Ch. 10. Glas. Col. Soc. (1825–1840).

  V. **Un. Ch. Can.** 1. Org. 2. Mem. 3. Mem. in Ont. 4. Pres. Ch. in Can.

 VI. **Bap. and Luth.** 1. Bap. Mem. 2. Luth. in Can.

VII. **Doub. and Men.** 1. Org. 2. In B. C. and Sts. 3. Mem. in Con. 4. Mem. of Men.

VIII. **Other Dem.** 1. Adv. 2. Breth. and U. B. 3. Chris. 4. Ch. of Christ. 5. Dis. of Christ. 6. C. S.

REVIEW QUESTIONS

How far did the power of Rome extend in the seventeenth century? Who made this possible? Whom else did this Society win over to Catholicism? Where did these Indians live? In what year did Jean de Brebeuf found his mission? Where? How far did the Jesuits extend their mission?

Which denomination first established a church in Canada? In which province was the Roman Catholic Church the most powerful influence? What is the total Roman Catholic population of Canada? of Quebec? of Ontario?

By what other name is the Church of England called? What were its outstanding characteristics in the early days? What is its membership in Canada? How many Anglicans are there in Ontario? British Columbia has a population of how many Anglicans?

Was the Christian Church in Canada free from the controversies in the church that were prevalent in the mother country? What were the branches of the Methodist Church in Canada? Name the five divisions of Presbyterianism in Canada. Who supported the Church of England in Canada? the Methodist missionaries? What society aided the Presbyterians in Canada between 1825-1840?

Name the denominations forming the United Church of Canada. What is its membership? Which denomination refused to join the merger?

What is the membership of the Baptist Church in Canada? How many Baptists are there in Ontario? in the two provinces of New Brunswick and Nova Scotia? Where in Canada are the greatest number of Lutherans found? Which province has the next largest number? Give the total number of Lutherans in Canada.

Who are the Doukhobors? In what part of Canada have they settled? Describe them. How many of this sect are now in Canada? State the number of Mennonites in Canada.

What other denominations prevail in Canada? Name each and give the number of each.

INDEX

Abelard, Peter, 145
Adventists, in Canada, 222
Albigenses, 141
Alexandria, 62
Ambrose of Milan, 98
Anglican Church, 220
Anglo-Catholic Movement, 179
Angora, capital of Turkey, 144
Anselm, 145
Anthony, early monastic, 88
Antioch in Syria, 30
Apollinarian controversy, 87
Apostles' Creed, 62
Aquinas, Thomas, 146
Arian controversy, 86
Asbury, Francis, 211
Athanasius, 86, 98
Augustine, St., 81, 100

Babylonian captivity of Popes, 113
Baptism, 44, 45
Baptist churches in America, 201-202
Baptists, in Canada, 221
Barbarians and Roman Empire, 94-98; conversion of, 98
Barnabas, 30-31
Benedict's Rule, 89
Benedictine monks, 135
Bernard of Clairvaux, 145
Bishops, growth of power, 59-61
Bishop of Rome, 90
Boniface VIII, 113
Brebeuf, Jean de, 219
Brethren, in Canada, 222
Byzantium, 82

Caliphate, abolished, 120
Calvin, John, 155, 168
Canada, churches in, 219-222
Canada, United Church, 190
Canossa, 111
Carey, William, 183
Carthage, 63
Cartwright, Thomas, 185
Catacombs of Rome, 68

Catholic Church, Greek, 105, 125, 144
Catholic Church, Roman, 40, 90, 105, 150, 156, 163, 193-196
Celibacy, 138
Chaledon, Council, 93
Charlemagne, 122
Charles V, Emperor, 124, 153
Christian Church (Disciples), 215-216
Christianity at end of first century, 44
Christians first named, 31
Christian Science, in Canada, 222
Christian Scientists, 218
Chrysostom, John, 99
Church: among the Gentiles, 34-40; condition of, under persecution, 67, 68; growth of, in early times, 68; of twentieth century, 190; union, 190
Church of Christ, in Canada, 222
Church of England, 220
Church of Scotland, in Canada, 221
Church of Scotland, union, 190
Churches: in Canada, 219-222; in United States, 193-218; National, 162
Cistercian monks, 136
Community of goods in early church, 25
Congregational-Christian Church, 199
Congregational churches: in America, 198-199; in Canada, 221; in England, 176
Constance, council of, 114
Constantine, Emperor, 73; Edict of, 49, 74; forged donation of, 108; successors of, 84; toleration of, 84
Constantinople: Council, 87; name changed, 82; taken by Crusaders, 82, 130; taken by Turks, 144

254 INDEX